LITTLE LONDON ADVENTURES & COCKNEY CURIOSITIES

CLARE NEWTON

"Sometimes curiosities are sitting right under one's nose. But even more peculiar, are the stories of old, passed down by family members, all sitting round a log fire and then into some crazy book such as this. Artist and photographer Clare takes you on a bizarre and hidden journey – cycling in and out the city gates and up and down the 'easel', mixing stories with latter-day visions of life, that often become invisible, amongst the bustle of the city's existence. This journey compares today's London to its bemusing roots with written historical trinkets, simply to amuse you too."

First Published January 2019
ISBN 978-1-912951-01-7
Limited Edition Hardback only

Artprints available to purchase
*https://happylondon.wixsite.com/press/***artprints**

HAPPY LONDON PRESS
Hybrid publishing for new talented authors
https://happylondon.wixsite.com/press

HappyLondon@gmx.co.uk

Come and Join our many fun events
from Dramatised evenings
to Beta-reader social gatherings

LITTLE LONDON ADVENTURES & COCKNEY CURIOSITIES

CLARE NEWTON

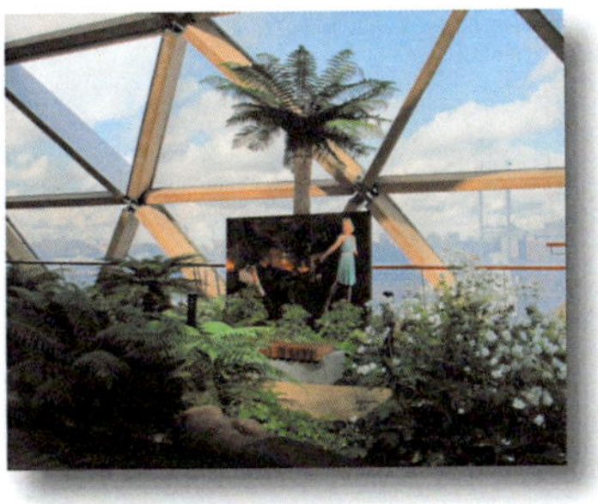

Contents for Curiosities

TUDOR SARCASM : *A man with a big nose*

HOW PURPLE WAS INVENTED IN SHADWELL

COULD IT HAVE BECOME PERKIN'S PURPLE?

MILE END WONDERS

THE NOTEBOOK

of Richard Newman of Mile End New Town

THE BLACKWALL TUNNEL HITCHHIKER

DICKENS AND THE CHINAMAN

CAUGHT IN THE JAWS OF A BENGAL TIGER

FORWARD

I am sure you have come to discover that London is a treasure trove of curiosities and artifacts. But before I came to live in east London, I didn't really consider there was anything of interest let alone of importance in its historical past. But how wrong I was.

Back in 2007 and the announcement of the Olympics coming to London. It was hinted that parts of Newham, would undergo a complete transformation, with the arrival of four spanking new sport centres and a giant stadium. Thus spurring me to jump on my bicycle and photograph the area, before it changed forever.

As I poured over maps, books and old newspapers, I discovered East London's extraordinary historical richness and the Victorian's insatiable appetite for innovation. Way back, when the world came beckoning at the door of London, via the river Thames, it was quickly followed by the rapid expansion of trade, merchants and immigration, and a fervent need for new inventions. Some have embedded themselves firmly in today's busy world; making them a necessity even today, we cannot do without.

This little book is not so much a picture book of where the events occurred, as this might be seen as a bit of a cliché. But rather an artist's journey of discovery of what lays under the surface of east London and its hidden photogenic gems.

The photographs are more a study about how contemporary regeneration, knits itself into the fabric of London's historical past. And whether modern buildings and relics have the ability to blend in or obliquely jar against them.

The artist invites you to join in the adventures and also find the illusive magic, that lingers amongst the shadows.

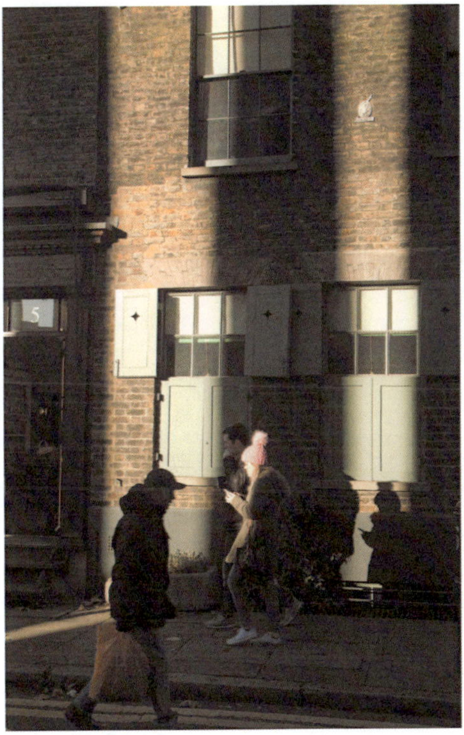

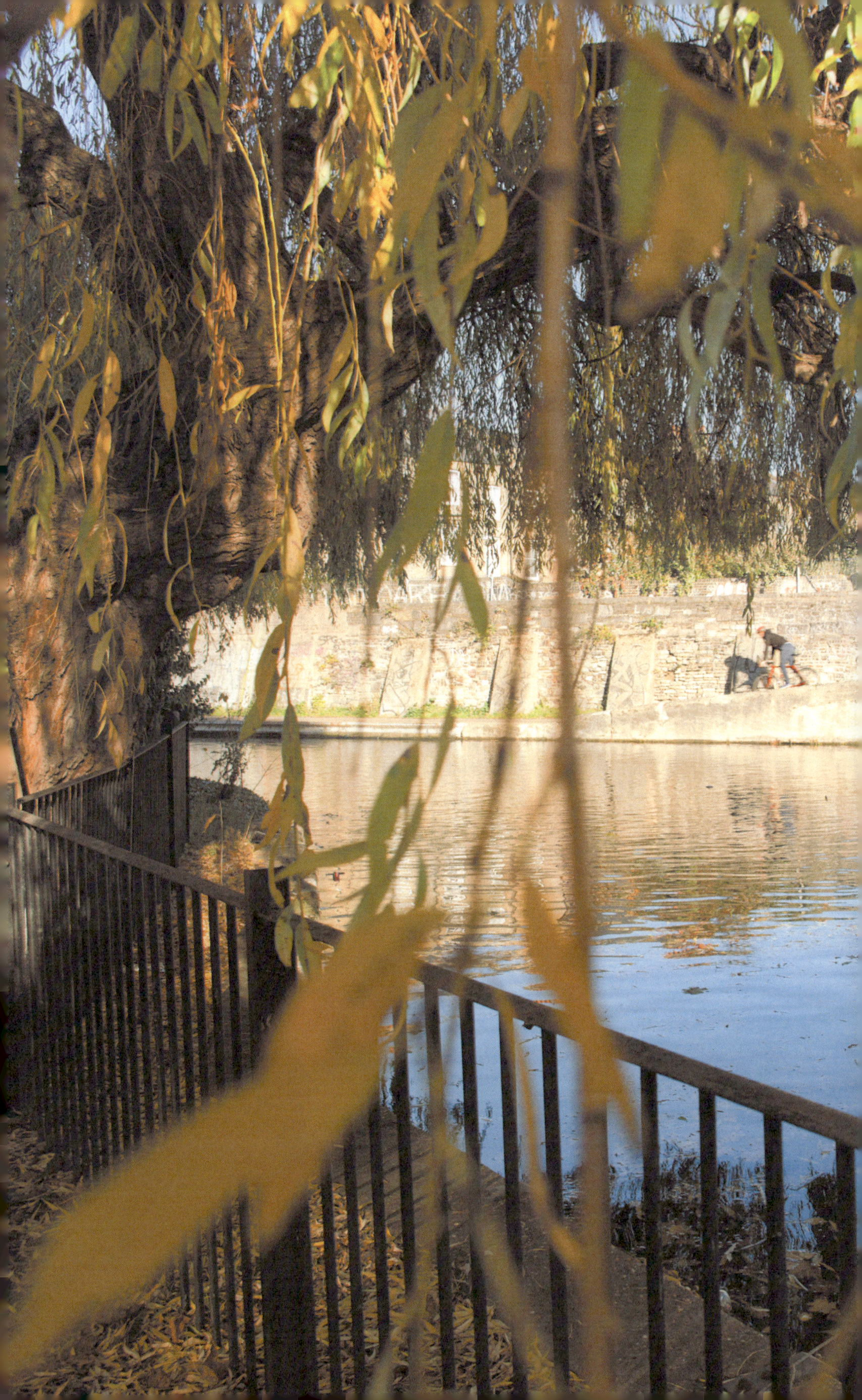

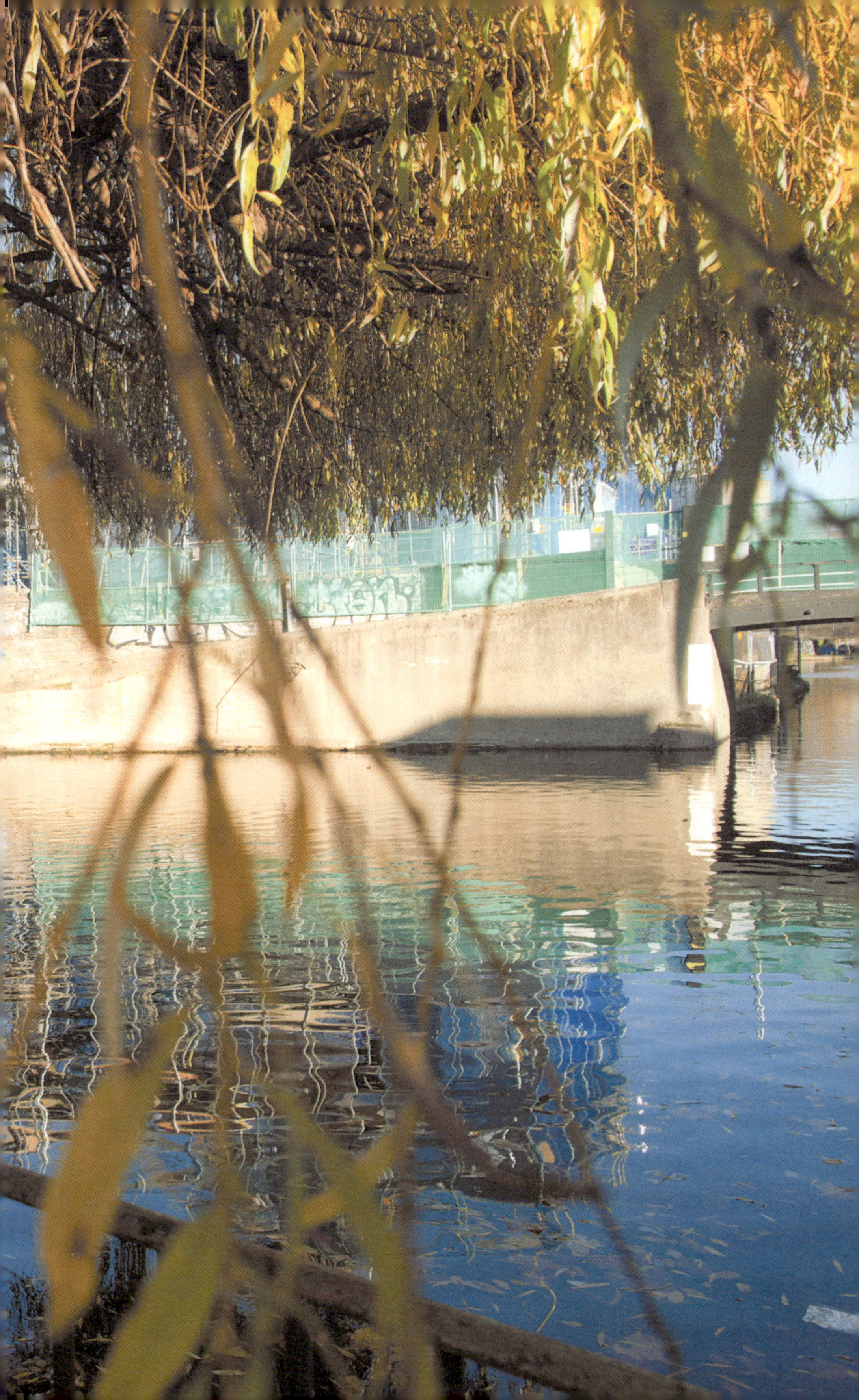

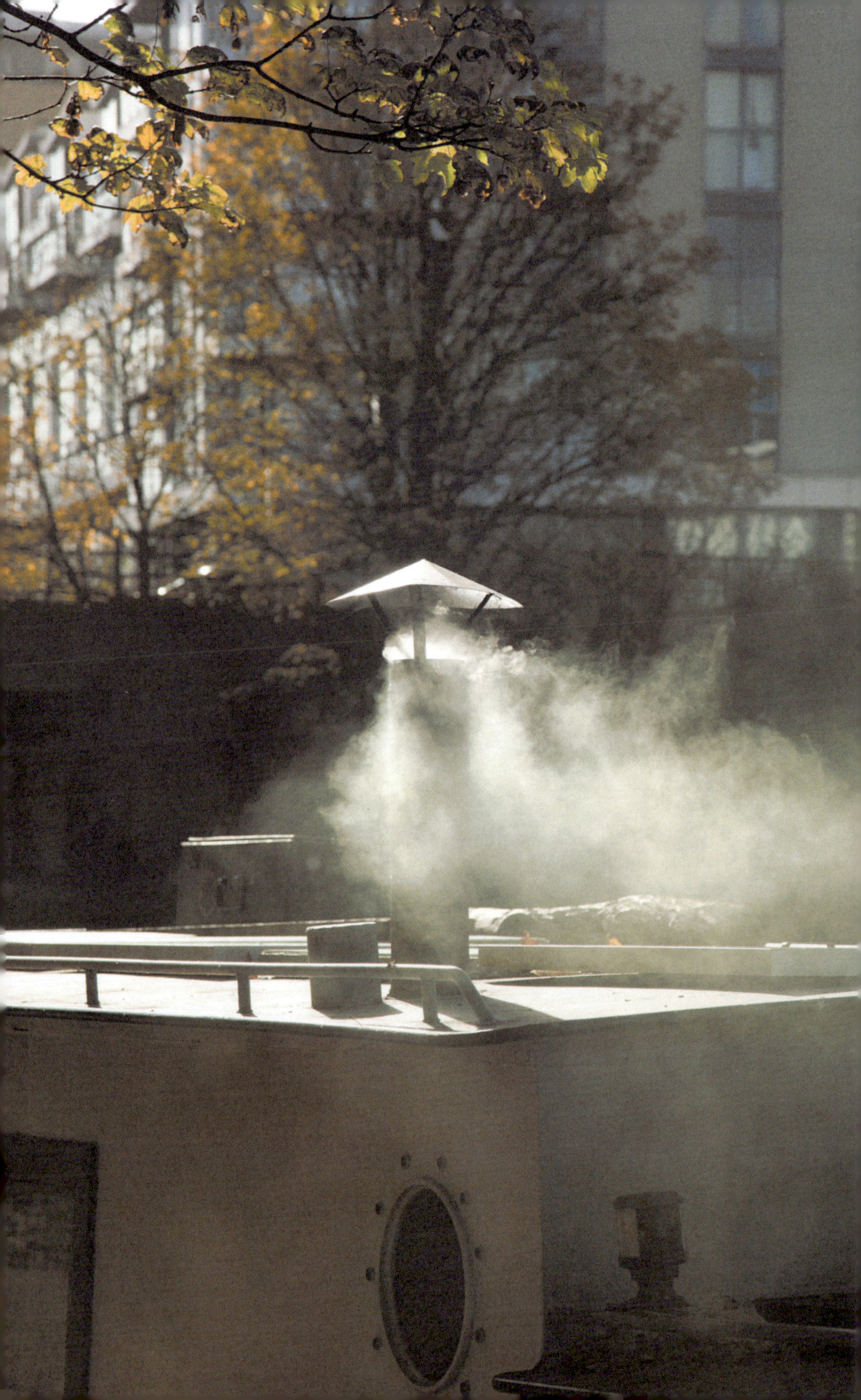

ORIGINS OF A COCKNEY

It's a curious thought, wondering where and how cockney slang started. Well it turns out that there are many trains of thought. This would mean the word could have first come into being in around 1362. Geoffrey Chaucer calls an ancestor a "cokenay," in "A Reeve's Tale," whom he construes to mean a man with an effeminate nature.

Whereas an Elizabethan linguist John Minsheu recounted an anecdote about a London child, who, after being taken to the countryside was informed by his father "that horses neigh" But the little boy heard a rooster and asked: "*Does the cock neigh too?*"

Shakespeare, at around the same time, used the word cockney in two of his plays. Once in King Lear, referring to the Cockney as an "idiot" exclaimed: "*O me! My heart, my rising heart! But down!*" the Fool retorts: "*Cry to it, Nuncle, as the cockney did to the eels when she put'em i'th'paste alive.*"

While in Twelfth Night, Feste (again a fool) meets Sebastian whom he mistakes his twin sister Viola for Cesario, as she is in disguise and says: "*I prithee vent thy folly somewhere else, Thou know'st not me.*" Feste, amused by Sebastian's pompous remark and answers: "*Vent thy folly! I am afraid this great lubber, the world, will prove a cockney.*"

With so many English words derived from the French the word crops up again with the French word 'coquin' meaning mischievous, rogue or scoundrel, which could refer to the unscrupulous market stall sellers.

Later in 17th Century Cheapside, the Cockney appears again this time referring to the Lord Mayor's working curfew, which allows all Cockney workers to down their tools at 9pm and thus the saying derived from the chimes of the curfew... "*Born within the Sound of Bow Bells*" and the purlieu of the Church of St. Mary Le-Bow.

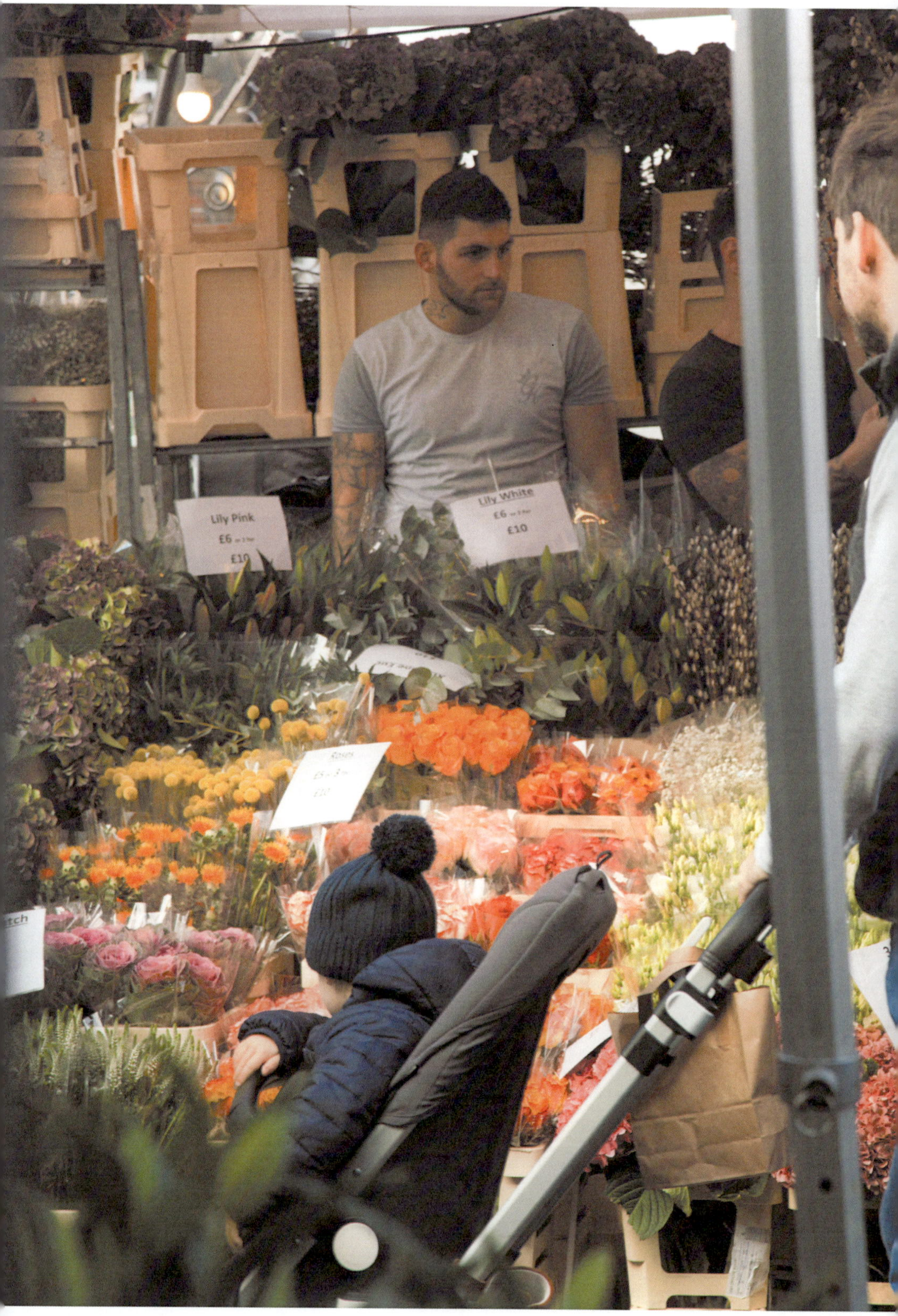
Lily Pink
£6
Lily White
£6
£10
Roses

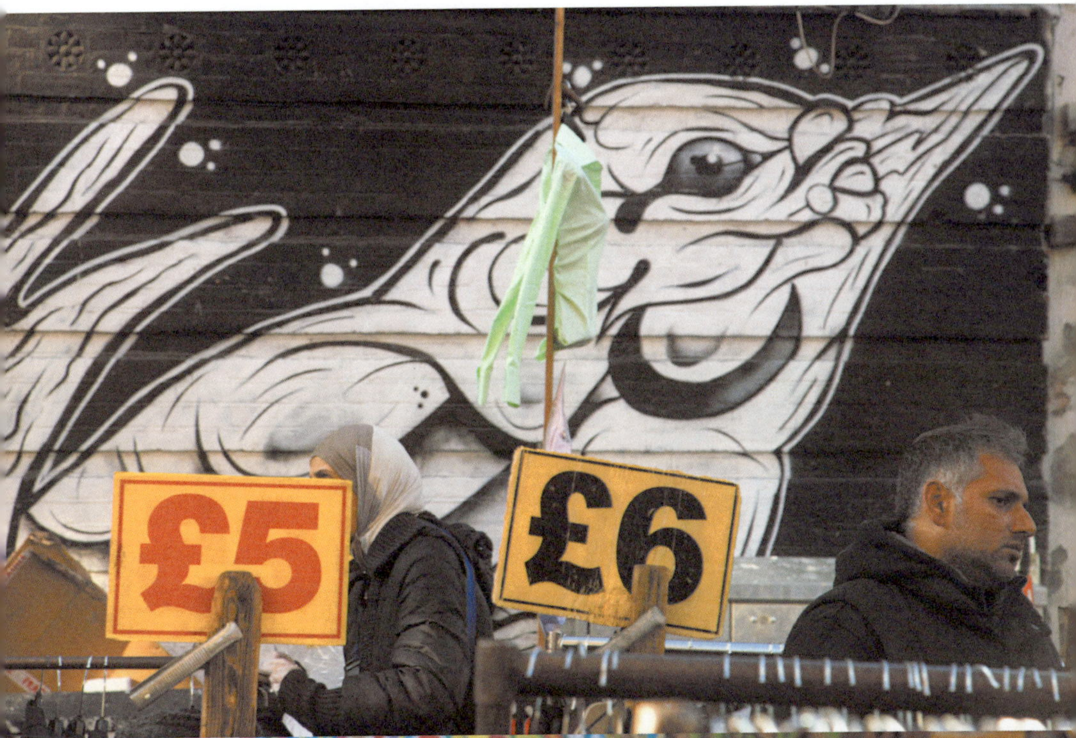
£5
£6

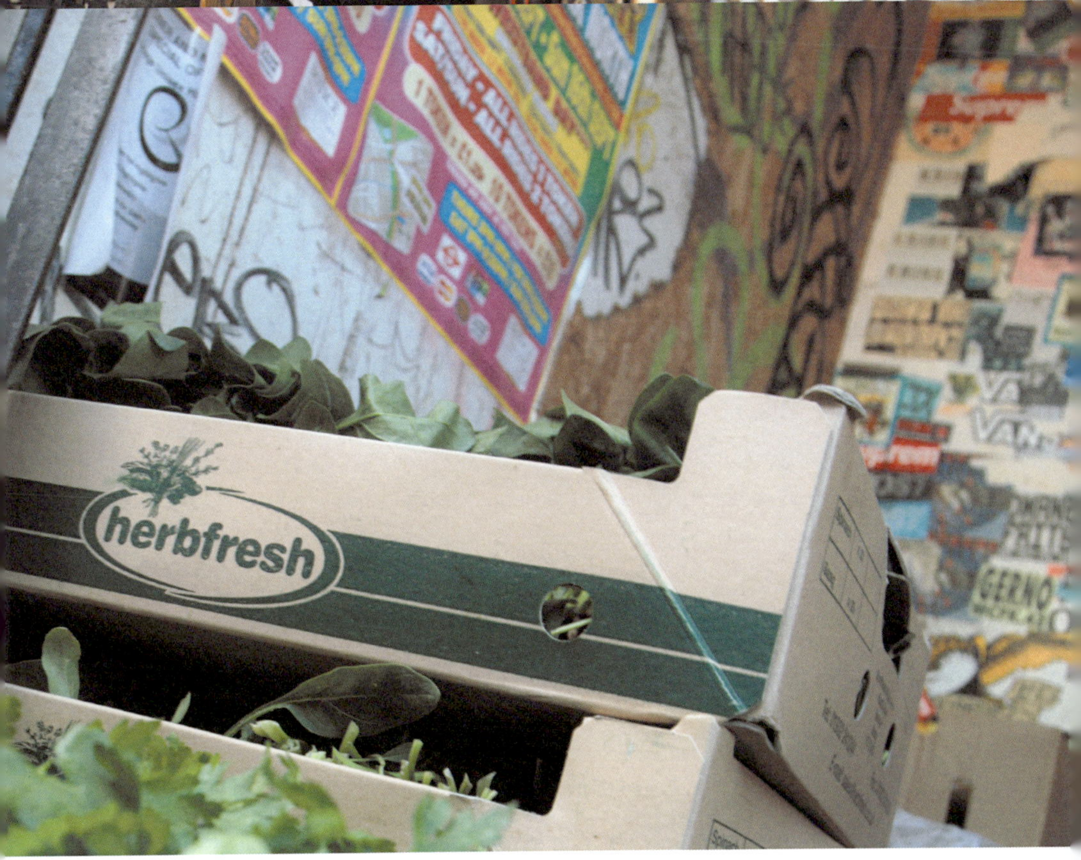
herbfresh

COSTER MONGERS AND COSTARD KINGS

Costermongers, the original Cockney, were early street sellers for fruit and vegetables, deriving their nickname from the Costard Apples, originally coined somewhere in the 1600s.

They bought fruit and vegetables from local farmers and growers, then hawked them from either fixed stalls or walked the streets with barrows, donkey carts, or 'shallows' (heavy trays balanced on their heads). It was feast or famine for Costers. Sometimes at the height of the fruit-picking season their earnings could average thirty shillings which they gleefully spent on flashy clothes giving an aura of success. Their motto, *"Spend it while you've got, tomorrow you might be brown-bread"*. But during the winter season or multiple wet days, they could starve, as there was nothing to sell – or it had perished.

Victorian Costermongers were at their peak, calling their chants to catch their customer's attention:
"Ho! Ho! Hi-ii Chestnuts, a penny a score",
"Three a penny, Yarmouth bloaters",
"Now's your time, beautiful whelks. A penny a lot",
"Penny a lot, fine Russets!",
"Come and look at 'em, here's toasters" (bloaters)
"I've a lovely bunch of coconuts" – Danny Kaye's song in the 1950s captured the spirit of the Calling Costers.

Often corrupt and sometimes obscene, these tough market-traders spoke a variety of cockney dialects, mixing back-slang and rhyme. This language, unique to the tightly knit community, was influenced by their mistrust for any form of authority; they would take any opportunity to pelt bricks at the local 'bobbies'. In one such story, a policeman impounded a barrow while another went to get help. Fellow costers slipped all the stolen fruit and hid it on a nearby, innocent, coster. They filled the barrow with builders' rubble, hidden beneath a blanket, and laughed while watching the police attempting to carry the barrow to the pound.

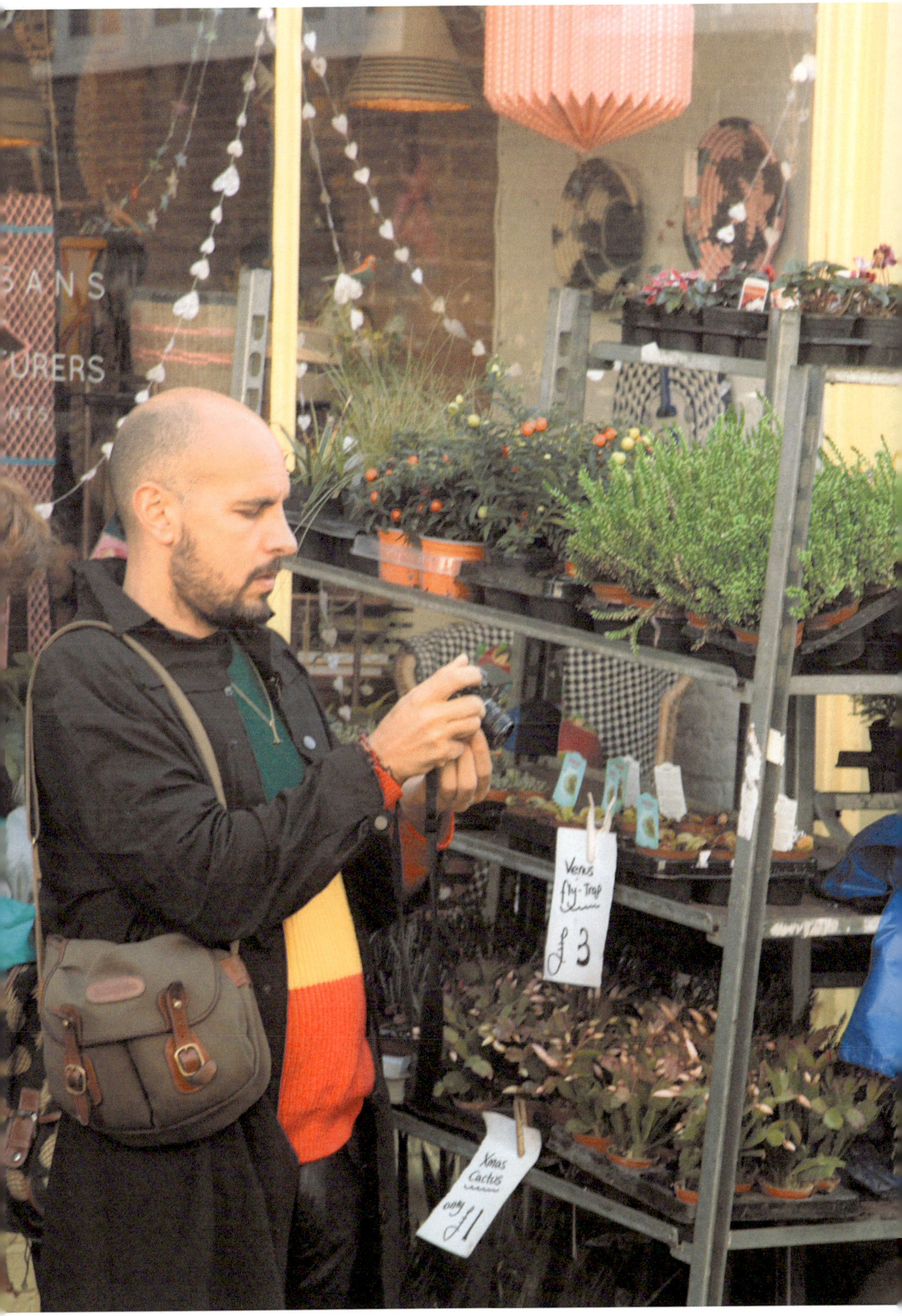
Venus
Fly-Trap
£3
Xmas
Cactus
only £1

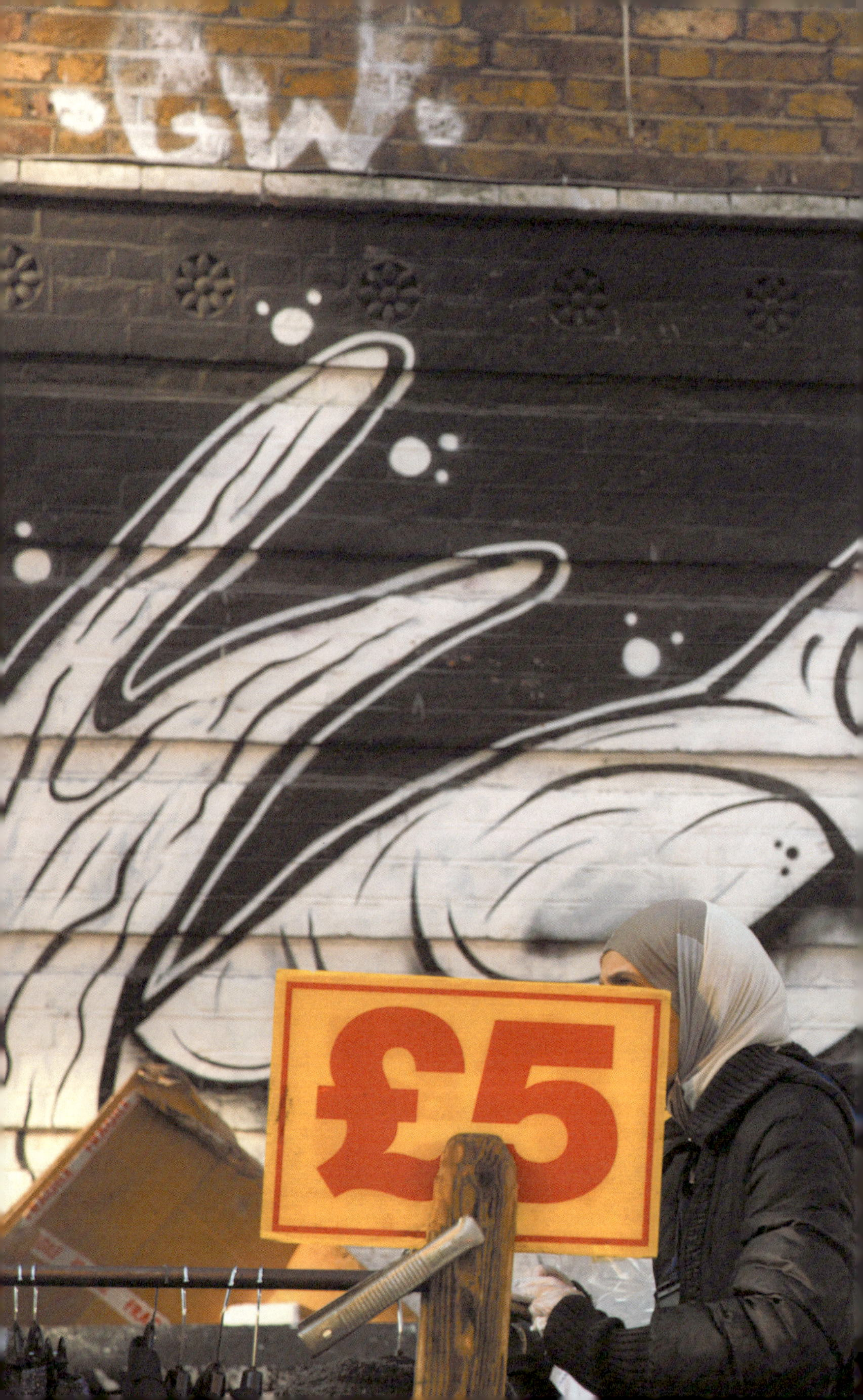
£5

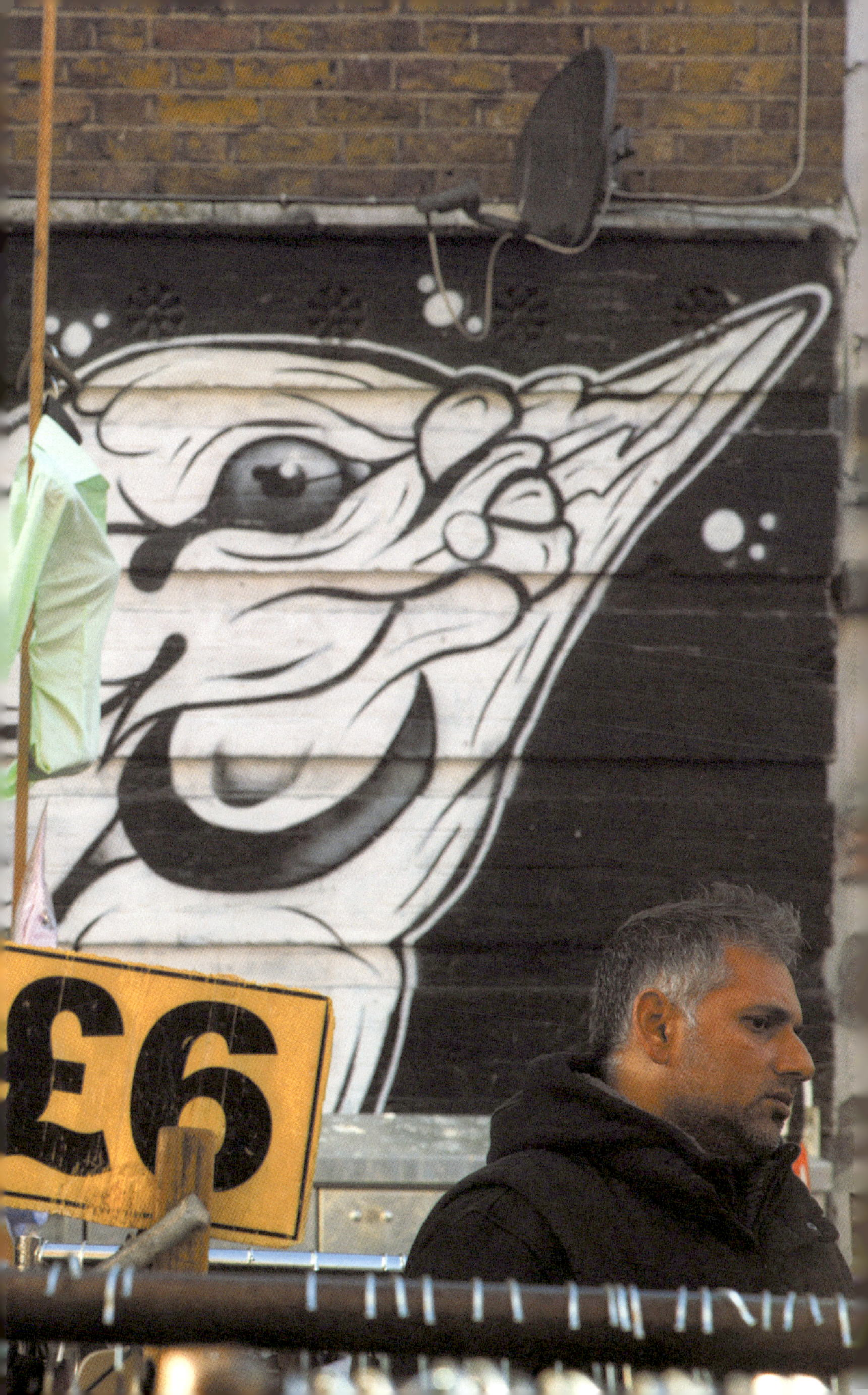
£6

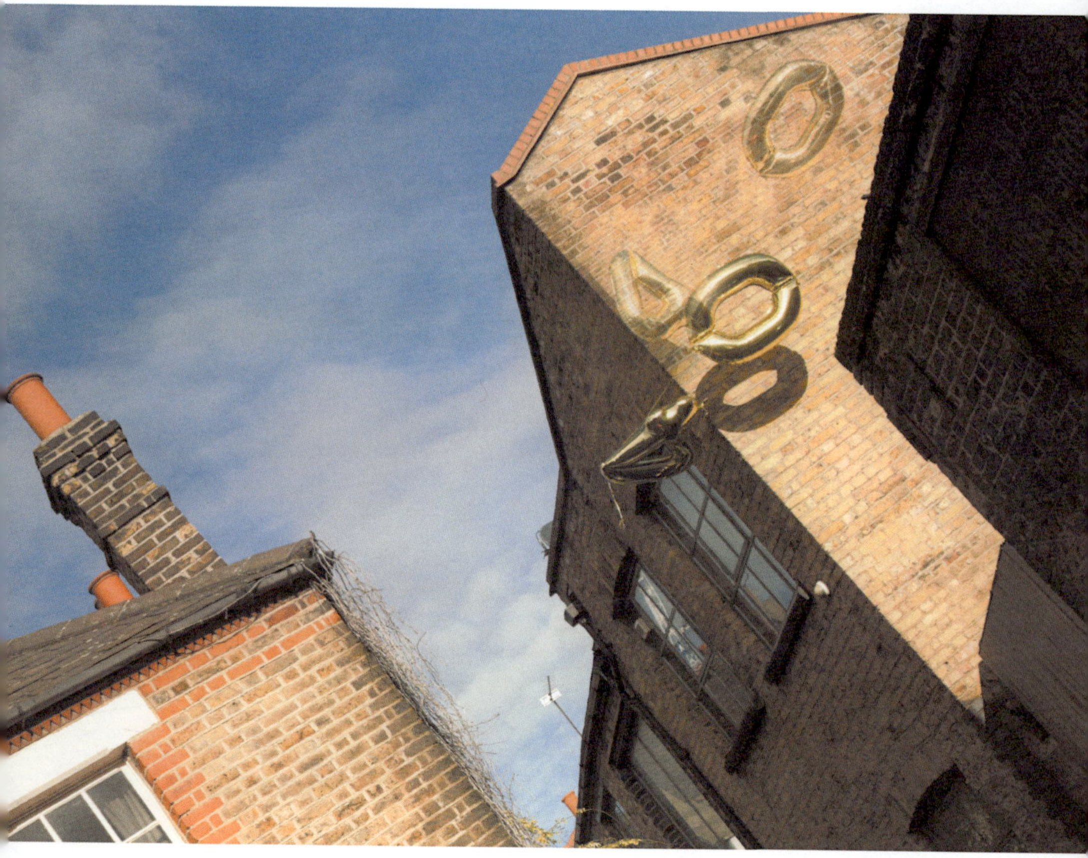

BACKWORD COCKNEY YOBS

Have you ever thought how language comes into being? Well, we can relate to its development, as we in this modern day of technology have invented a new lingo called 'Text-Speak', shorthand words and sentences which has come about from our early mobile phones. The full alphabet was condensed onto 9 keys, making it laborious to send long-winded texts. Back in the Victorian times, when winter seasons produced virtually no fruit and veg to sell, life was extremely hard and eking out a living from perishable goods was a highly risky business and prone to extreme poverty. It is said by some that the tradesmen, the Costermongers, invented the secret language to help warn each other of law enforcers, or unlucky well-to-do pedestrians straying in unknown territories who might be a foolish purchaser.

The construction of the lingo started out as "Back slang" the spelling of words backwards – something we still use today and know well – YOB is BOY. However, there are a few others we use, rhyming slang – we have fun with – adding our own matching sounding words. Here are some you know and are familiar with:

"'Aving a ***Butcher's Hook*** *" – for Look*

*"****Trouble and Strife****" – for Wife..."My trouble-and-strife called from the left-in-the-lurch to tell me that she's gonna for a spot of Ruby Murray" – Church, Curry*

"Would you ***Adam-and-Eve*** *it?" – Believe*

"Are you making ***Barney Rubble*** *again?" – Trouble*

"We sat and had a jolly good old ***Rabbit and Pork*** *– Talk*

"I forgot all my ***Sausage and Mash*** *– Cash!"*

*"****Fat Boy Slim****" – for Gym (remember the pop group too?).*

*"****Giraffe****" – Laugh... "You're 'avin a Giraffe, mate!"*

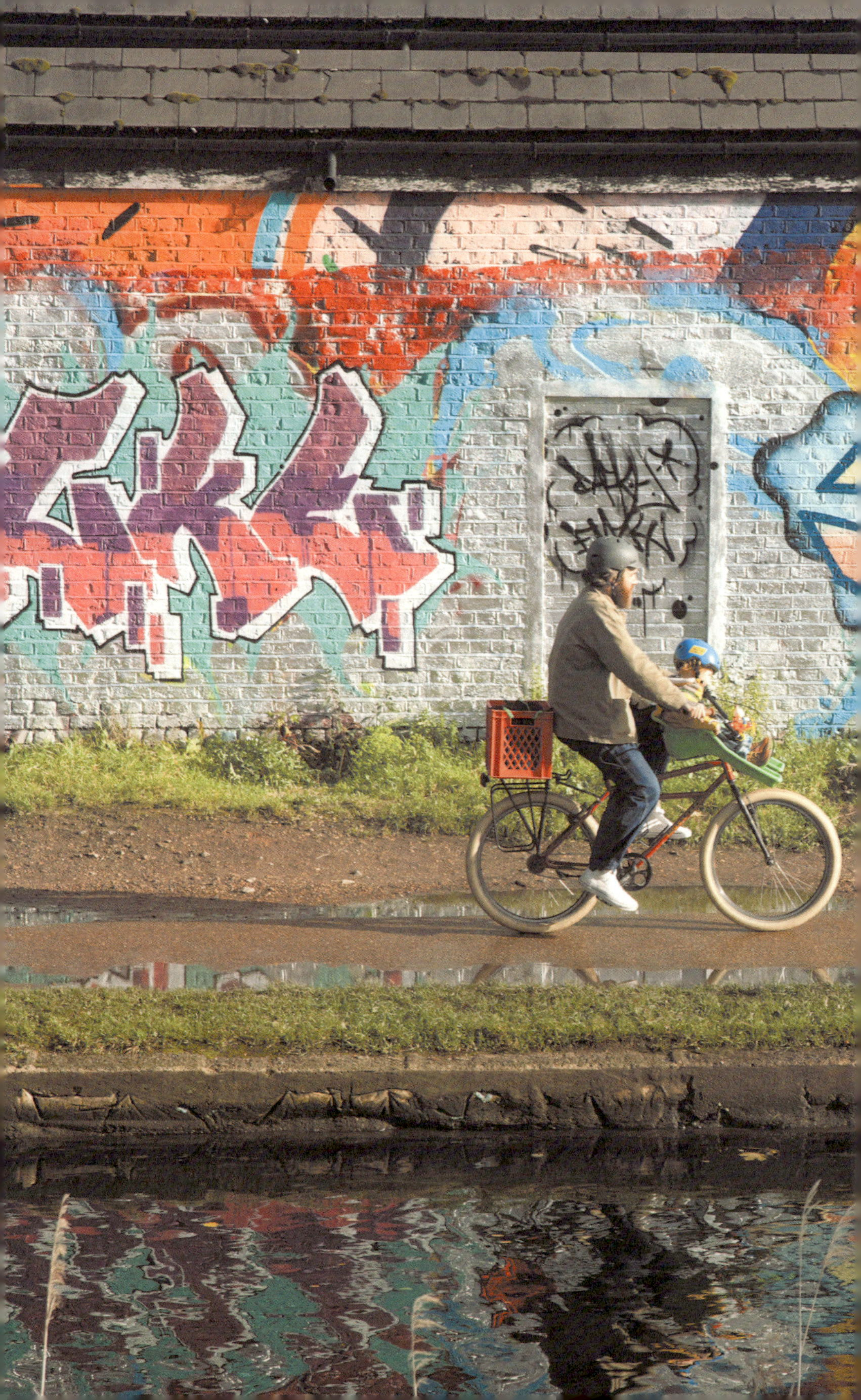

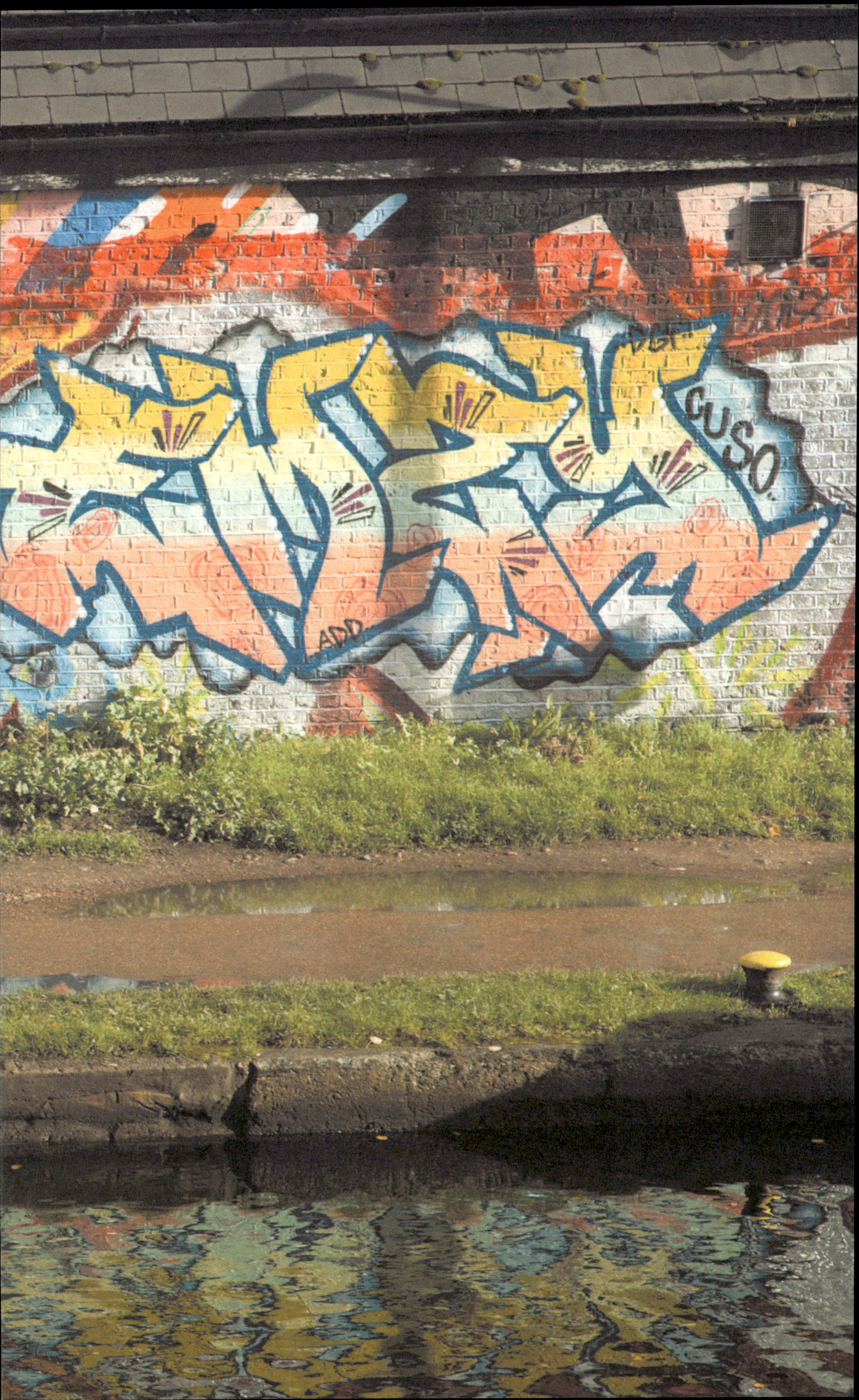
CUSO.

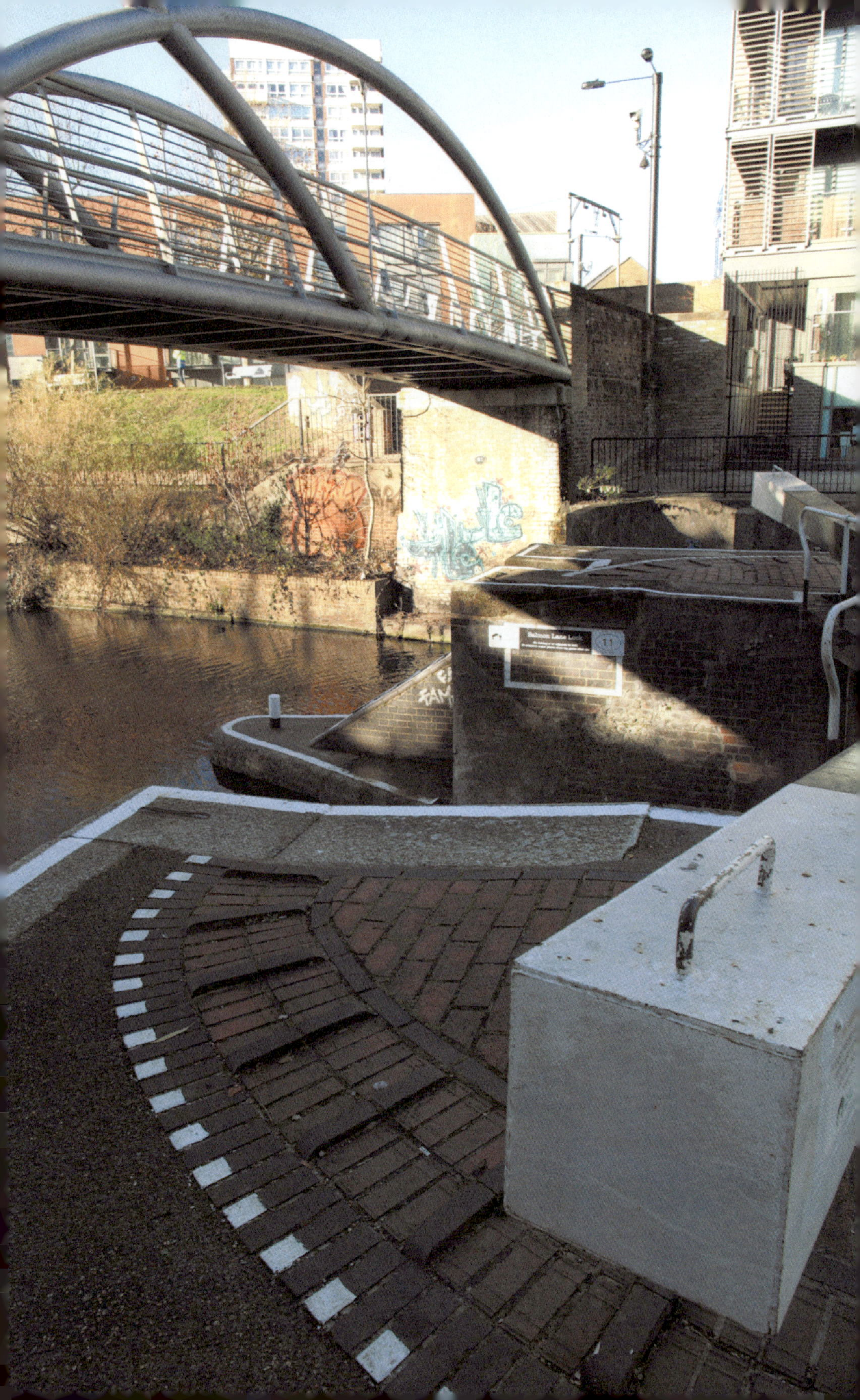
Salmon Lane Lock
11

"THE MASTER OF SUSPENSE" IN SALMON LANE

At number 175 Salmon Lane lived Mr & Mrs William Hitchcock, who owned a fish and chip shop. Each night the husband and wife team sold slightly spicy battered cod to disguise the taste of potentially spoilt fish. Their business was built upon the surplus fish, which failed to sell at Billingsgate Fish Market, once the largest fish market in the world.

These hard working parents enrolled their 11yr old son, Alfred Hitchcock into an extremely strict Catholic school, St. Ignatius College for boys, on Stamford Hill, just north of Hackney. According to author Gary Giblin, Hitchcock was pupil number 343. The intense disciplinarian education, heavily influenced Alfred in his film making, with many interviews revealing: *"all that I know about suspense and fear I owe to the Jesuits... and sitting outside the Headmaster's office. Even the threat of corporal punishment was worse than the actual experience"*.

After studying draughtsmanship and advertising, in 1919 Hitchcock became the editor of a newly launched magazine 'The Henley Telegraph'. The first issue published his short story entitled "Gas"... *The door stood at the head of a flight of stairs — stairs that creaked with age, as she endeavoured to creep down — then she heard the sound of drunken laughter and shuddered — surely this was — No, not that! Anything but that!"*

It was when in 1920, an American film company announced it was opening a studio in Islington, that propelled Alfred into the seismic world of transforming imagination into reality through film. And by 1929 Alfred had adapted and directed his first film "Blackmail". Where a shopkeeper's daughter kills a rapist, but is blackmailed by the detective. The film started as a silent movie, but very quickly became a 'talkie' due to its popularity in horror.

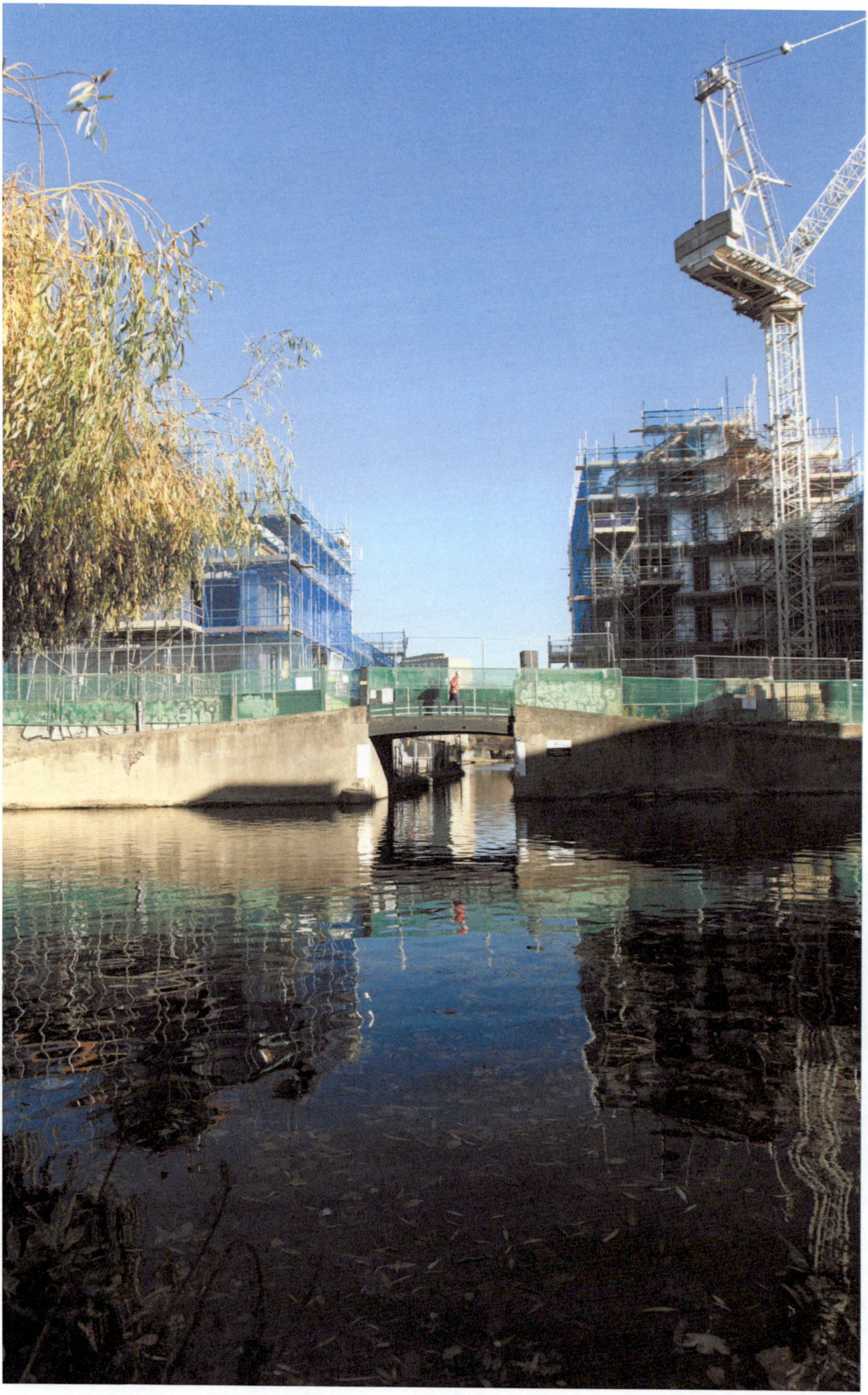

DUCKETT'S CANAL

The smallest canal becomes the shortest lived

Just behind Victoria Park, in the heart of East London, lurks one of the shortest canals ever built – at just over half-a-mile long. It was the brainchild of a local entrepreneur, Sir George Duckett. He thought he would capitalise on the congestion of narrow boats that collected around Old Ford Lock, from either the River Lee Navigation or the Limehouse Cut, both trying to access the River Thames at either side of the tidal gates.

The waterways were the essential trunk roads of the 19th Century industrial revolution, carrying the heavily laden narrow boats that linked manufacturers of the North to the global seafaring merchants who docked in the trading district of City of London.

Sir George Duckett persuaded the government of the day to grant an Act of Parliament, on 17 May 1824, that gave him Royal Assent to build a short connecting canal – the Hertford Union – linking the Regent's Canal to the River Lee Navigation. Its sole purpose was to ease the congestion of narrow boats that needed to enter the Thames, speeding the operation to meet the great merchant ships and deliver or collect the cargoes from around the world.

Sir George Duckett enthusiastically raised an astonishing £50,000 to cut the canal trench. His inspiration was that he would charge a shilling for every boat that passed through his single lock gate and thus quickly redeem his investment within the year. Unfortunately, in the grand scheme of things, the competitive rival's interconnecting canal – the Limehouse Cut – would loose at least 50% of its income from bargees. The Cut was owned by a wealthy enterprise, The Grand Union Company, with connections to the Prince Regent. And with their ownership came the water pumps at Limehouse Lock that returned the down flow of water back up the system to maintain the constant movement of transport.

The advantage was quickly used to great effect.

Within a month, trade wars soon emerged between the rival canal owners – and one dark night three barges laden with clay mysteriously offloaded their shipment and deviously dammed the entrance to Sir George Duckett's canal, preventing narrow boats' access – and the flow of water to refresh his single lock. It wasn't long before his canal dried up.

To add insult to injury, the rivals made it impossible for George to sell the canal, as they refused to remove the dam, so the whole venture closed in just one year.

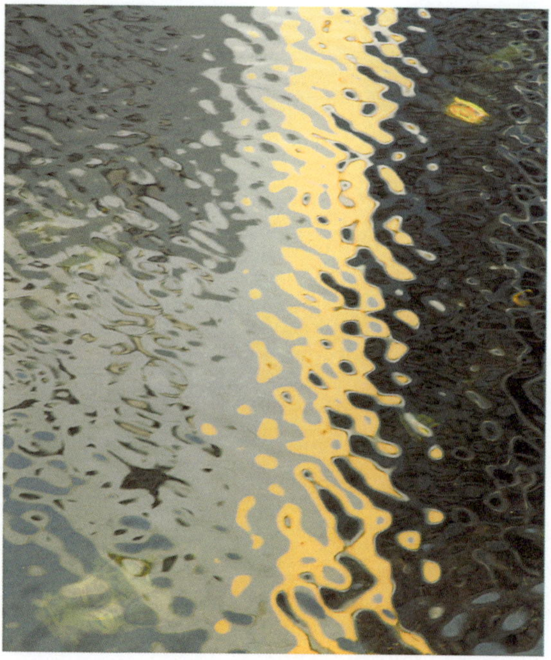

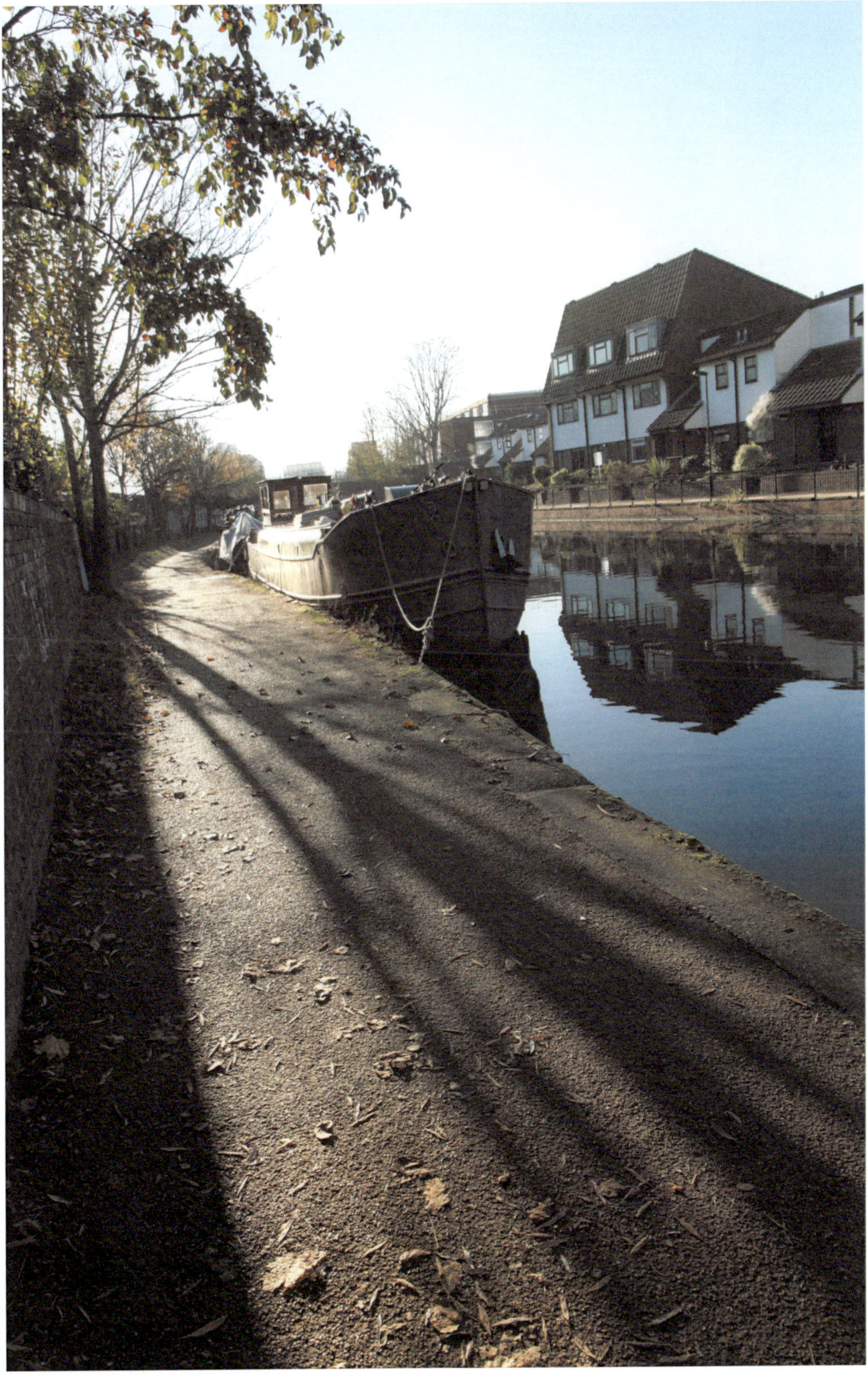

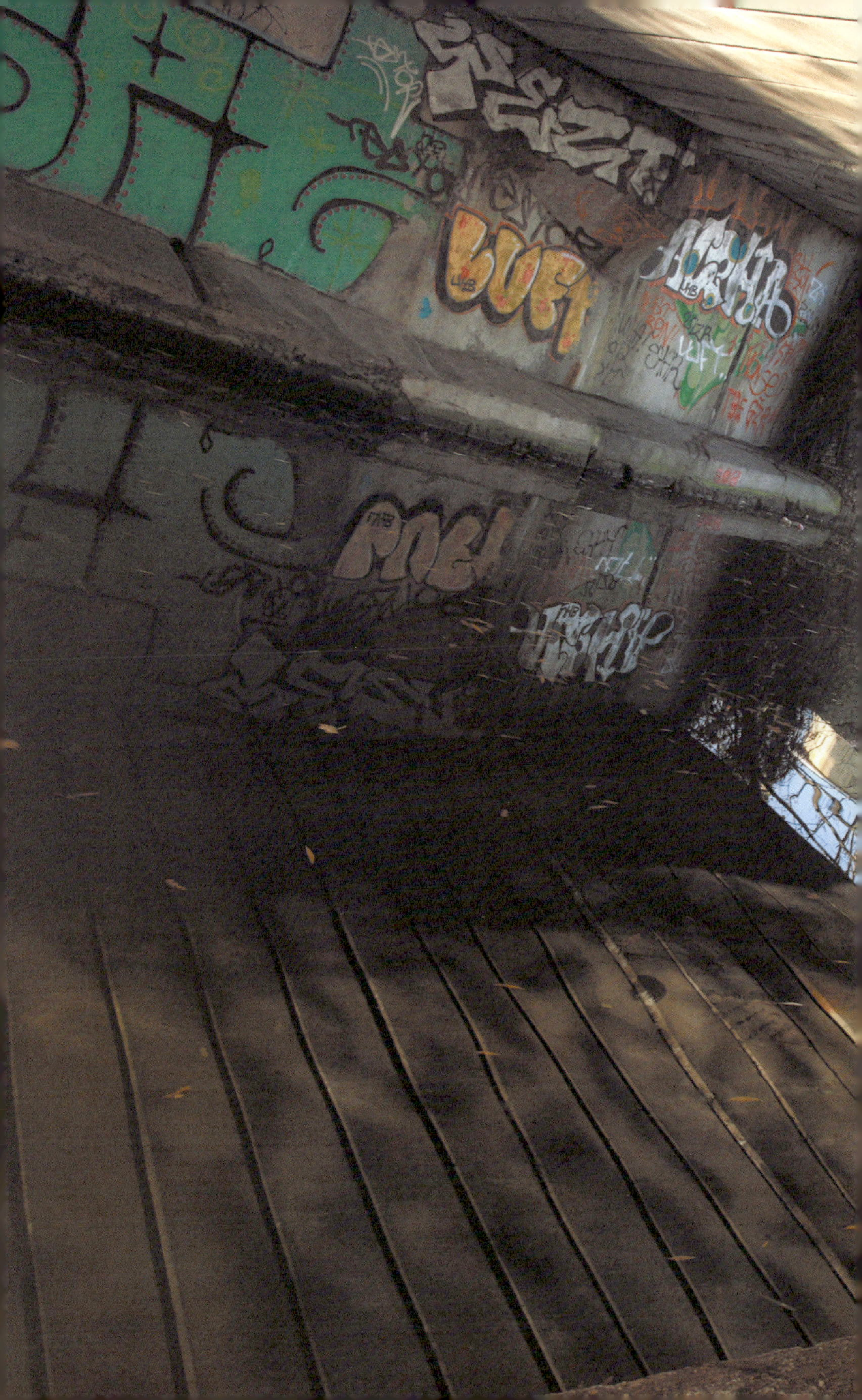

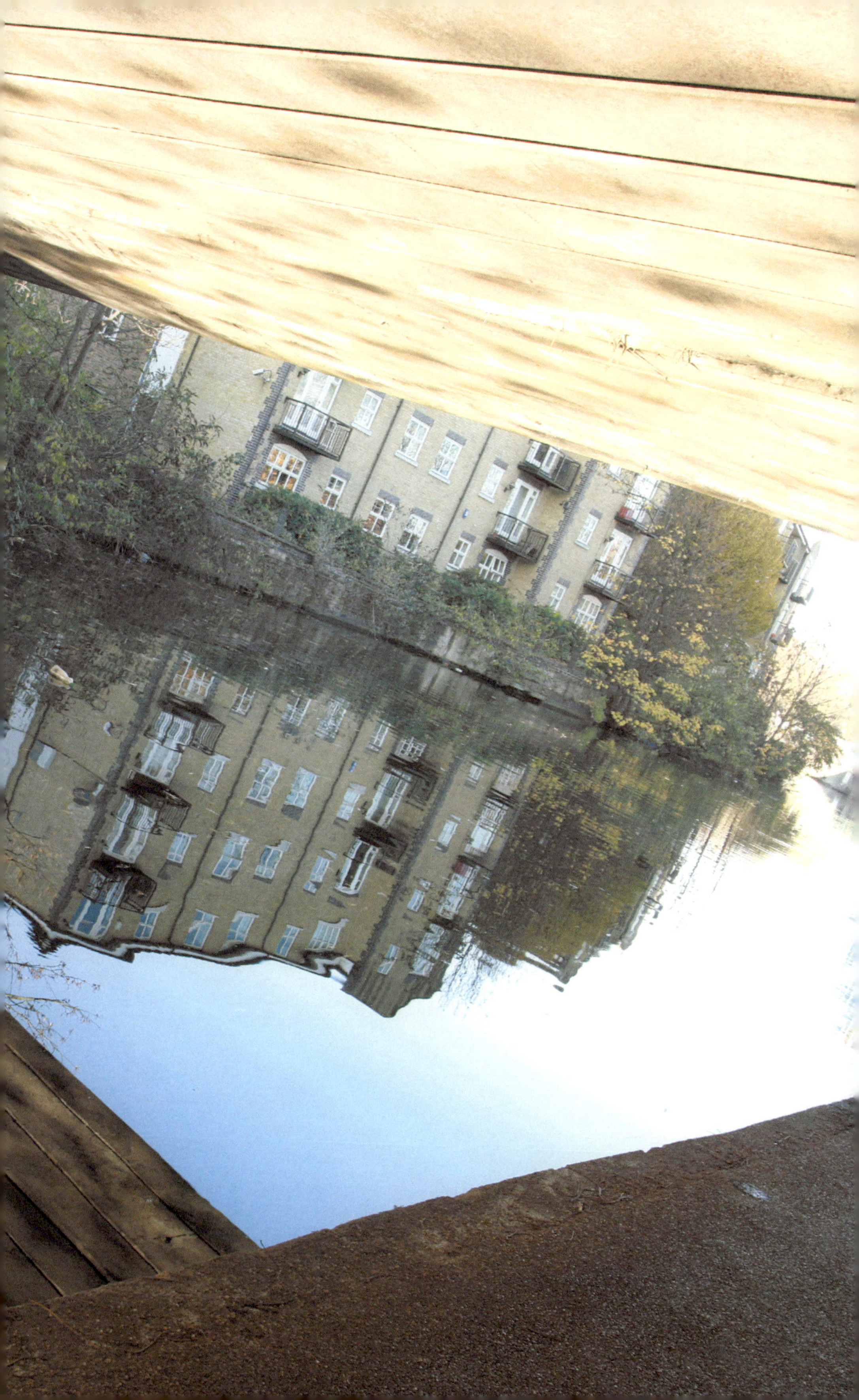

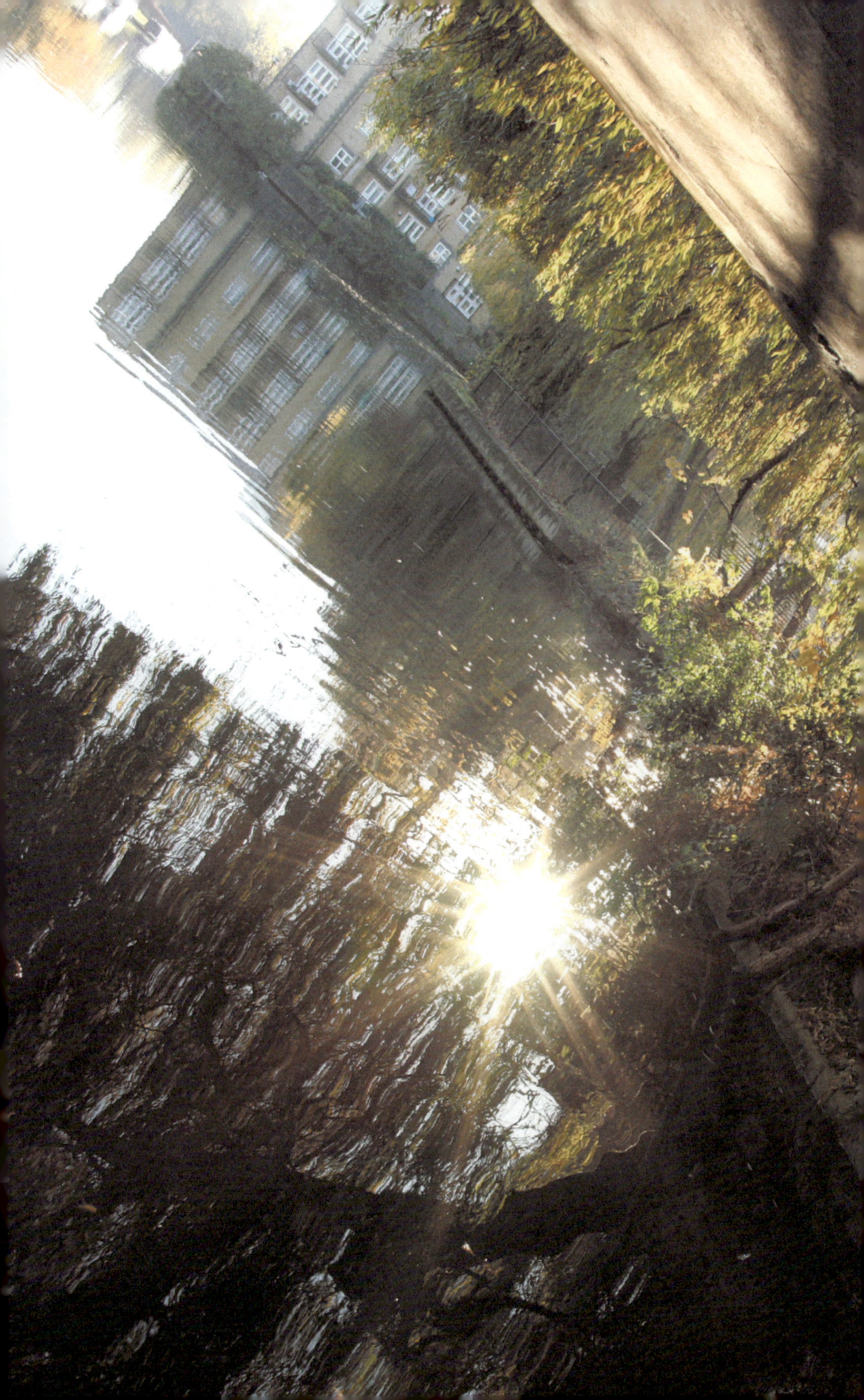

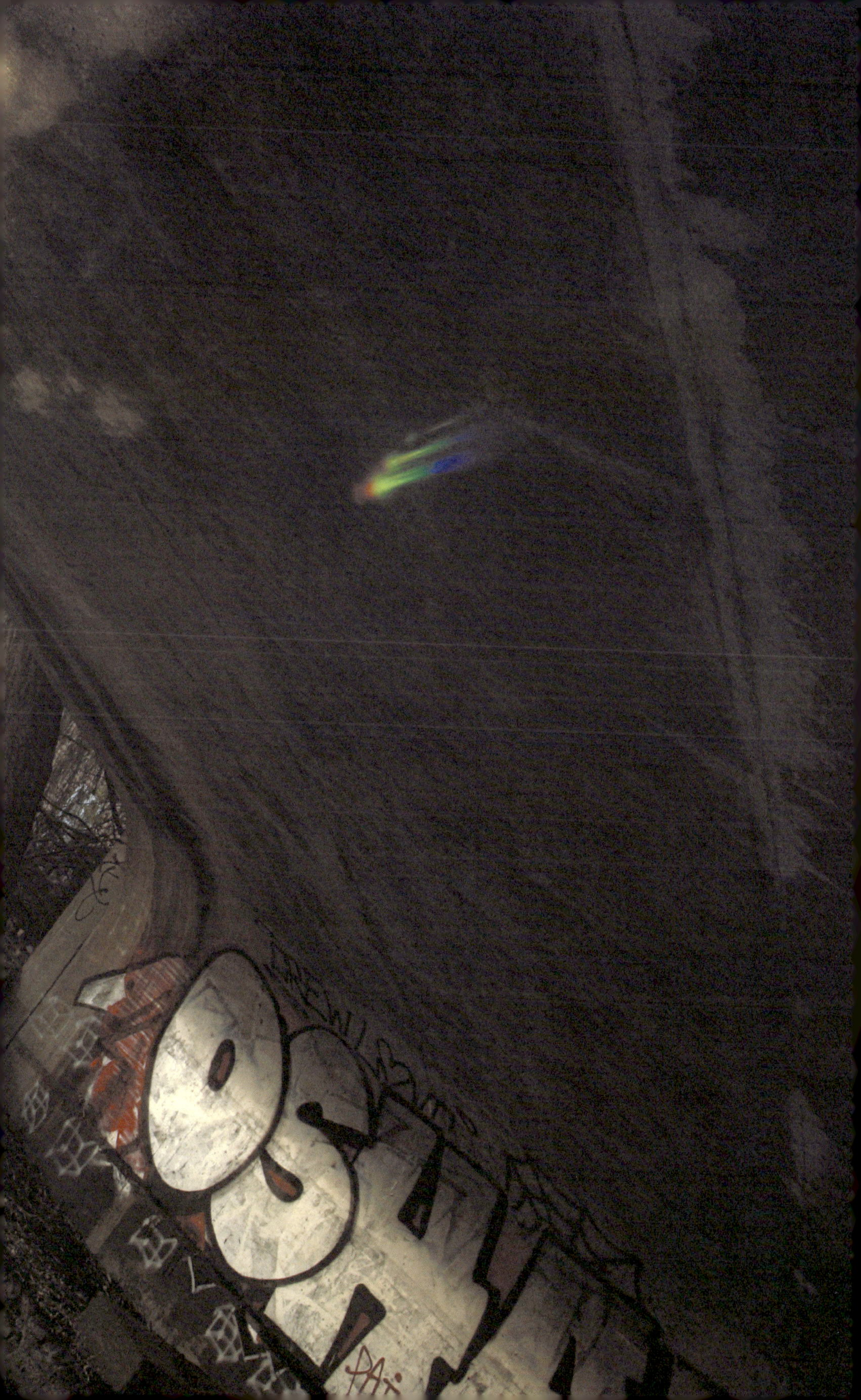

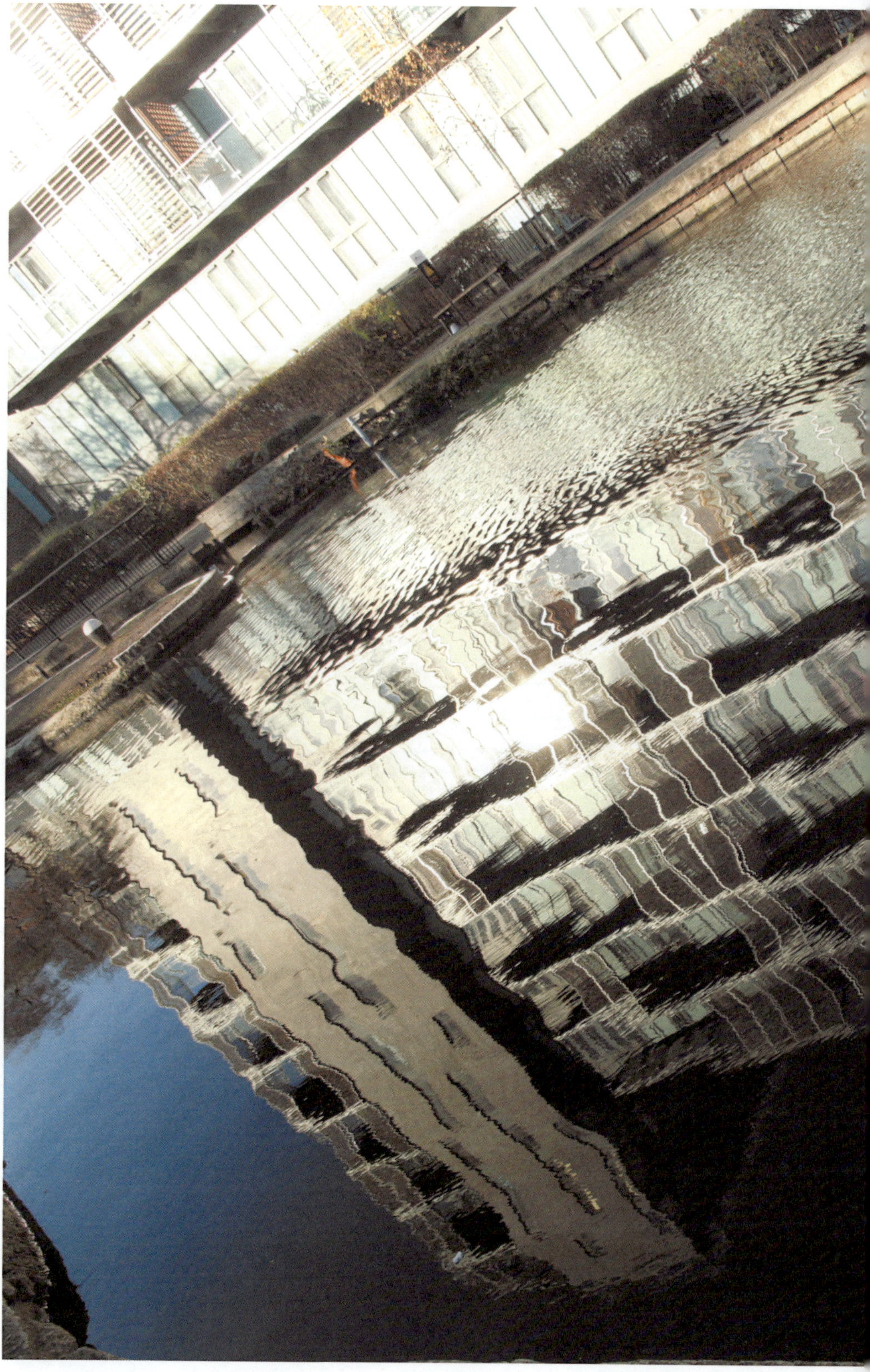

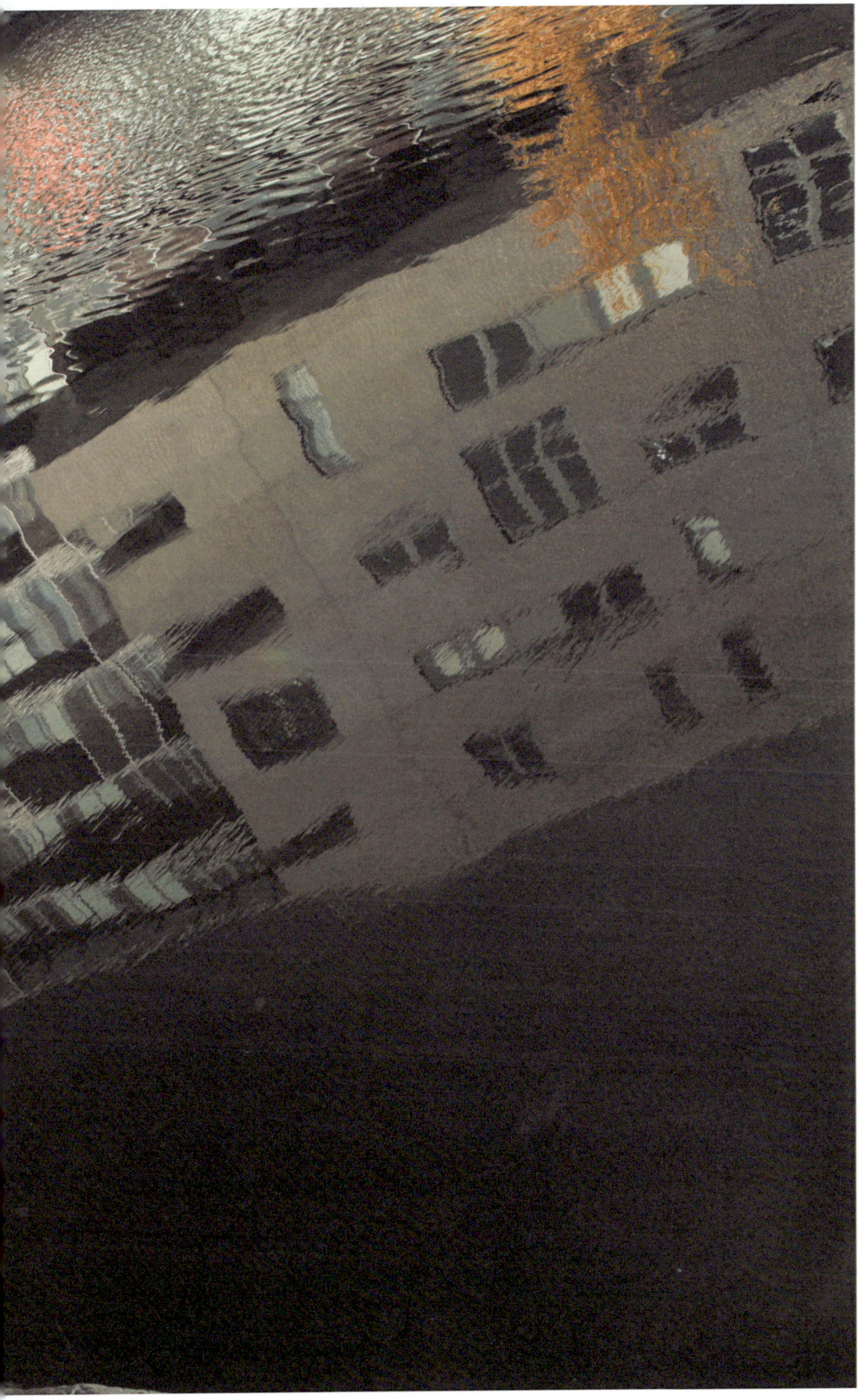

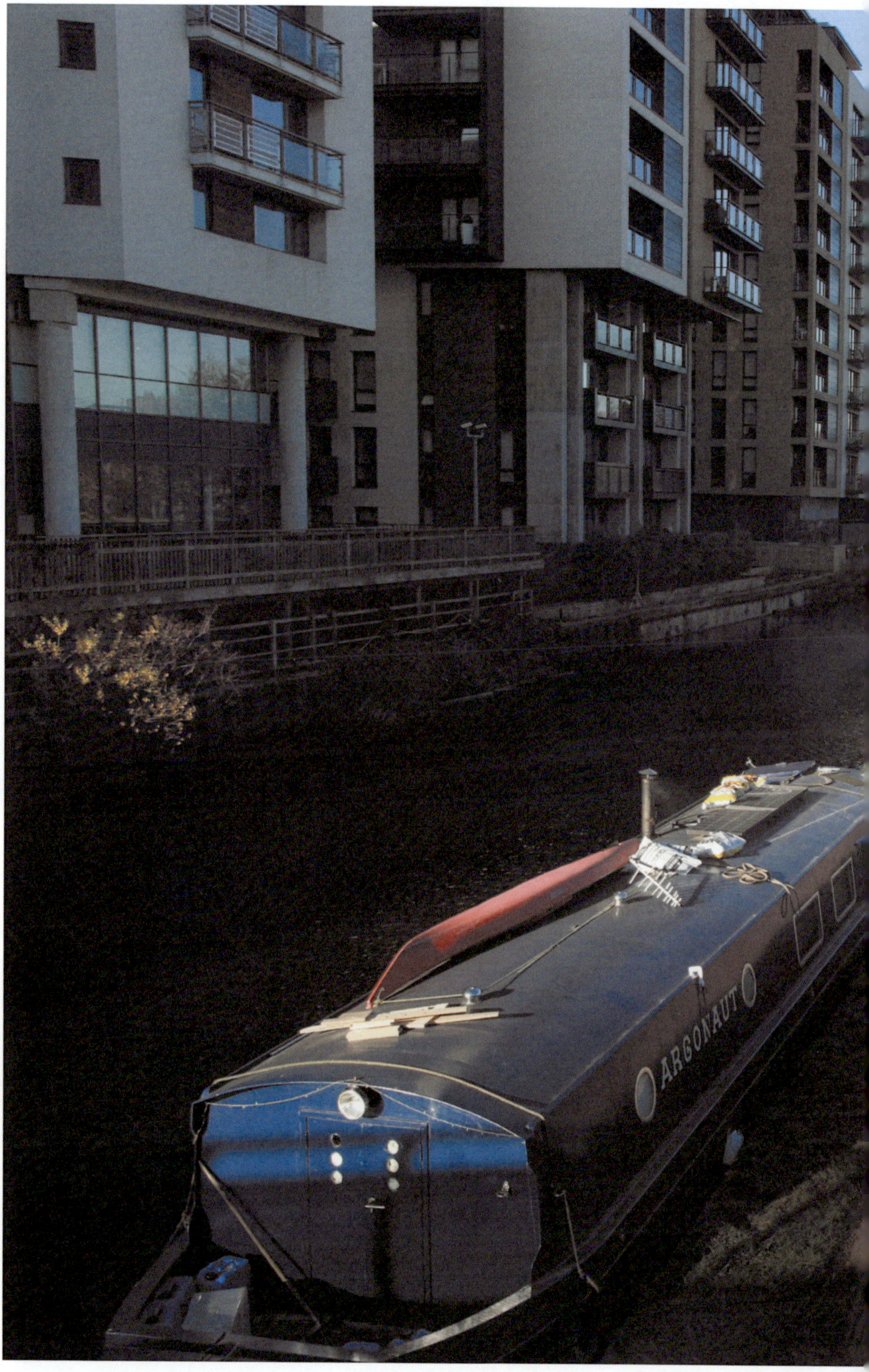
ARGONAUT

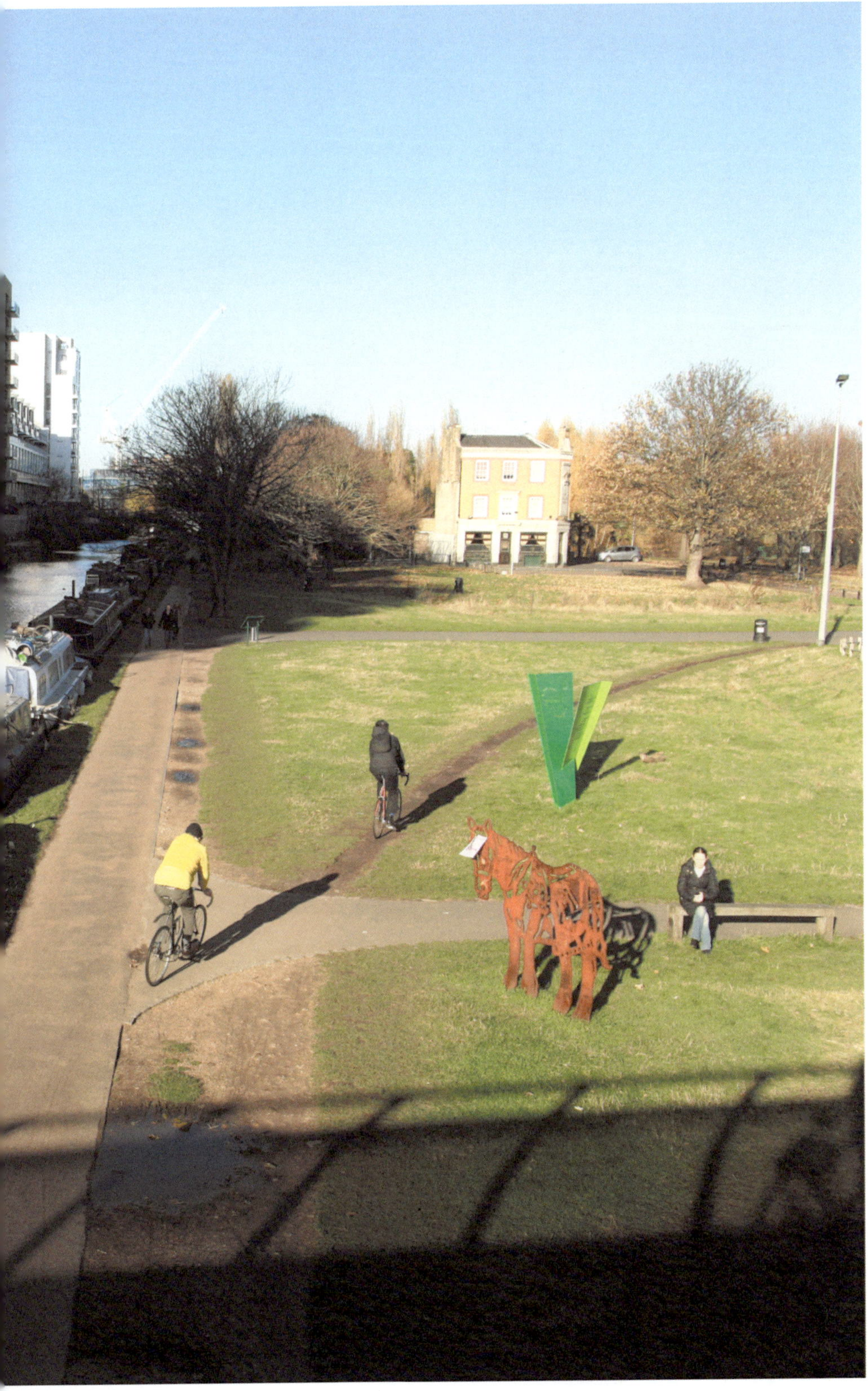

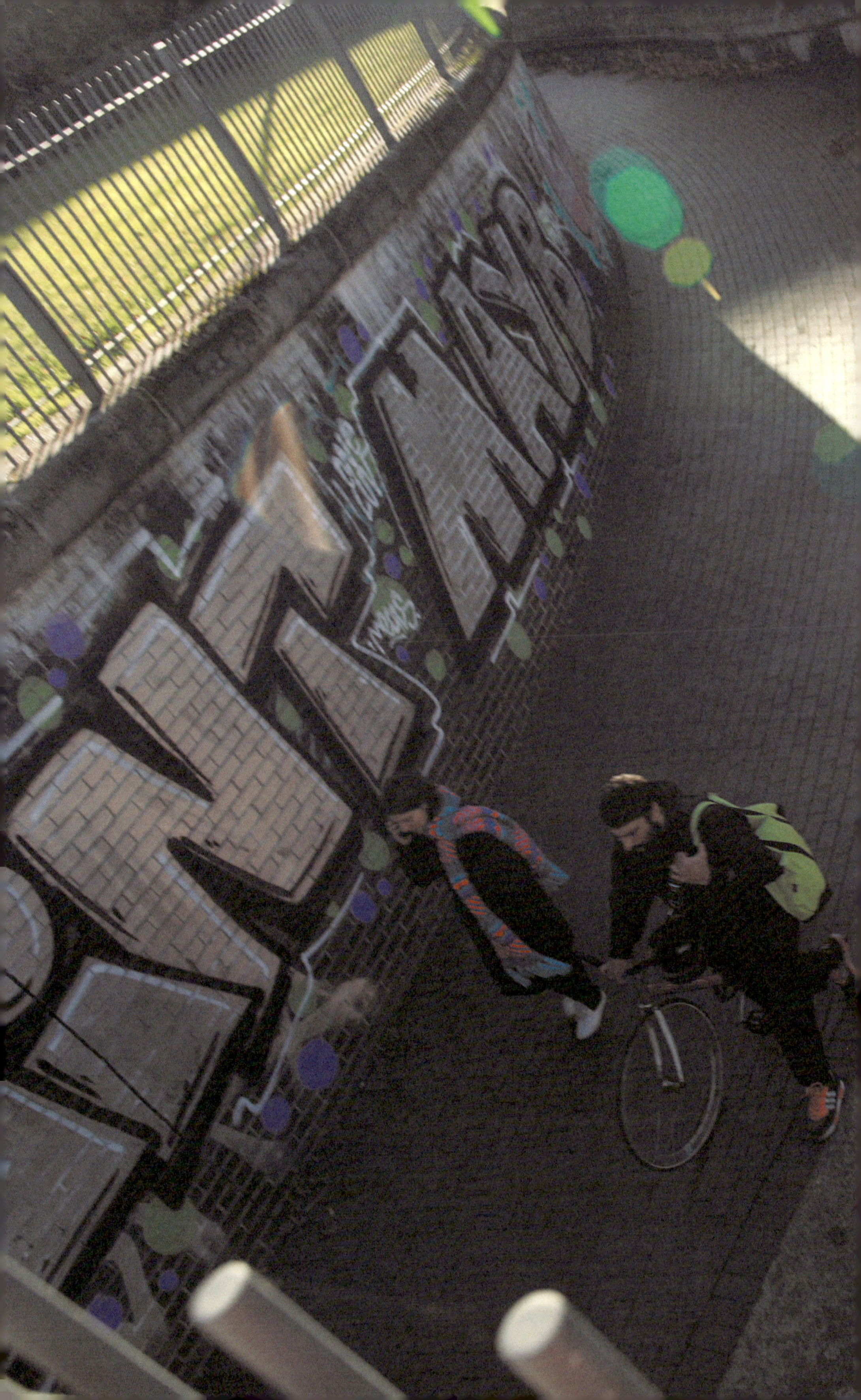

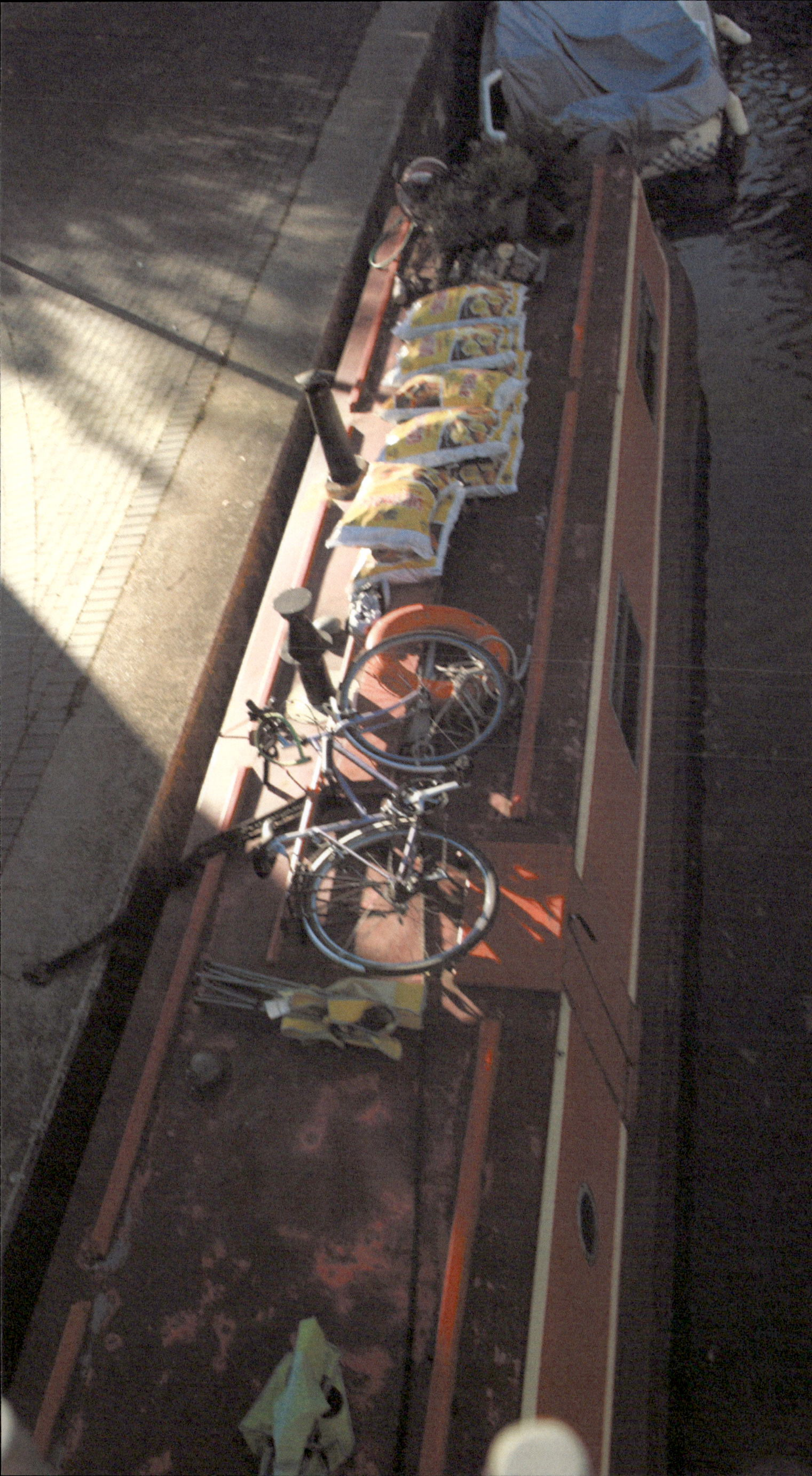

MERRY JANE OF SHOREDITCH

In 1476, Sir Thomas More exclaimed Young Jane to be *"the merriest, proper and most fair"*. Miss Jane was the daughter of a wealthy merchant in Cheapside and, at the tender age of 16, she was married off to a prospective goldsmith, William Shore, whose business in Lombard Street showed great promise.

But alas, even his wealth didn't match her lavish upbringing and her need for finery and expensive dresses to uphold her position in society. It wasn't long before she drew the attentions of King Edward IV, *"Fore a proper wit had she and can rede well and write, merry in company and quick in answer, without disport"*.

The King took special pleasure in her company and fell in love with this enchanting lady and openly made her his mistress. Jane moved residency to the King's palace where she could continue living in luxurious greatness, entertaining courtiers. But all good things come to an end. Edward's death on 9 April 1483 left Jane in a precarious position. She quickly realised that if she was to avoid the cruel disgrace of court, she would need to appeal for a new Protector. A variety of 15th century chronicles reveal two rival suitors; Thomas Grey, Marquess of Dorset – and Edward's closest friend – and his Chamberlain, William, Lord Hastings.

Jane took up Hastings' offer of attachment. However, the evil words of a jealous poet, Drayton, reached Edward's brother, Richard the Crookback, who seized the moment to dispose of Edward's disgraces and publicly shame the sinning harlot. Beheading Lord Hastings started his reign of treachery, causing the Bishop of London to put an open penance on poor Jane and parading her through the City's streets – until finally, some would tell, she fell dying in a ditch – Shoreditch.

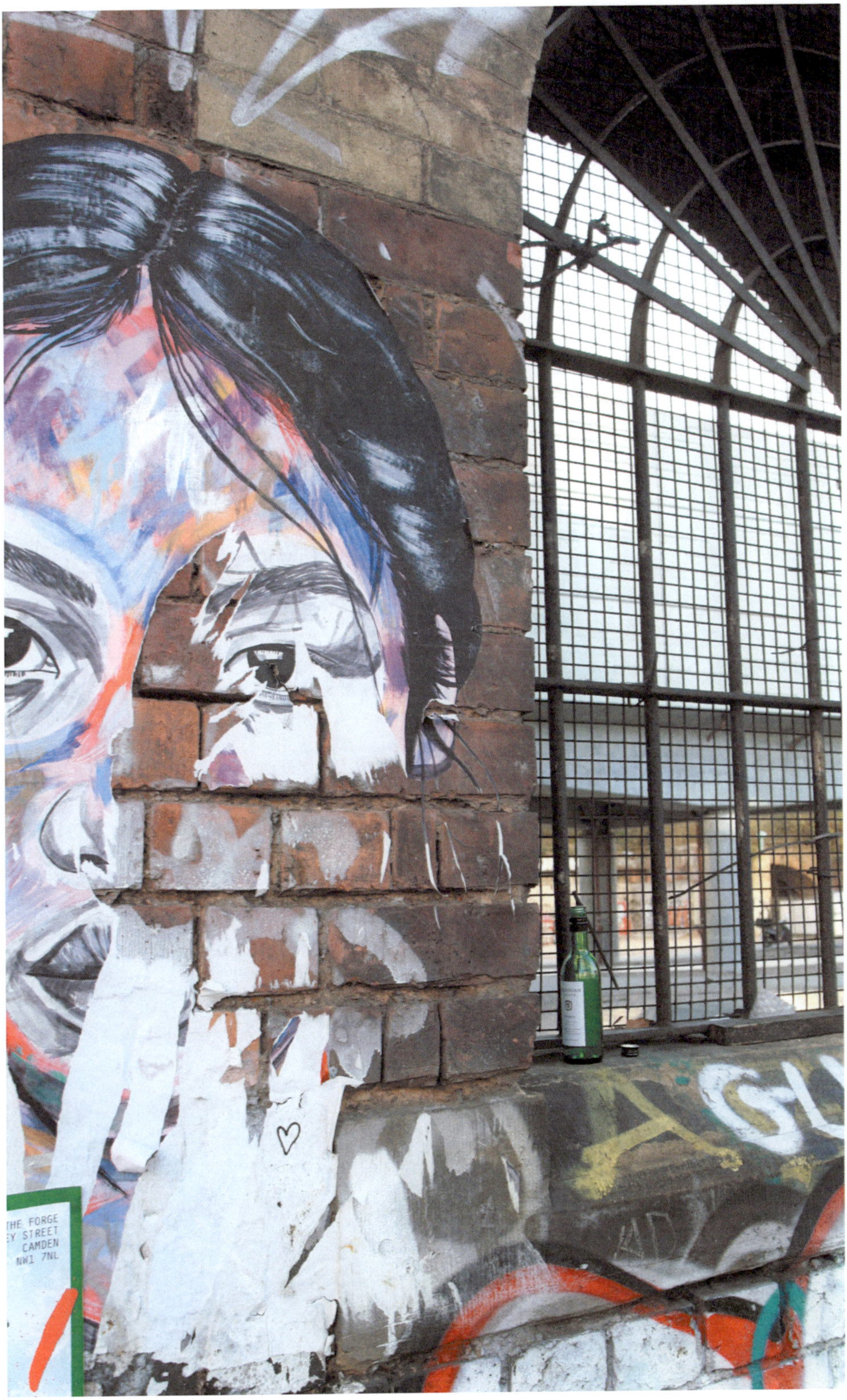
THE FORGE
EY STREET
CAMDEN
NW1 7NL

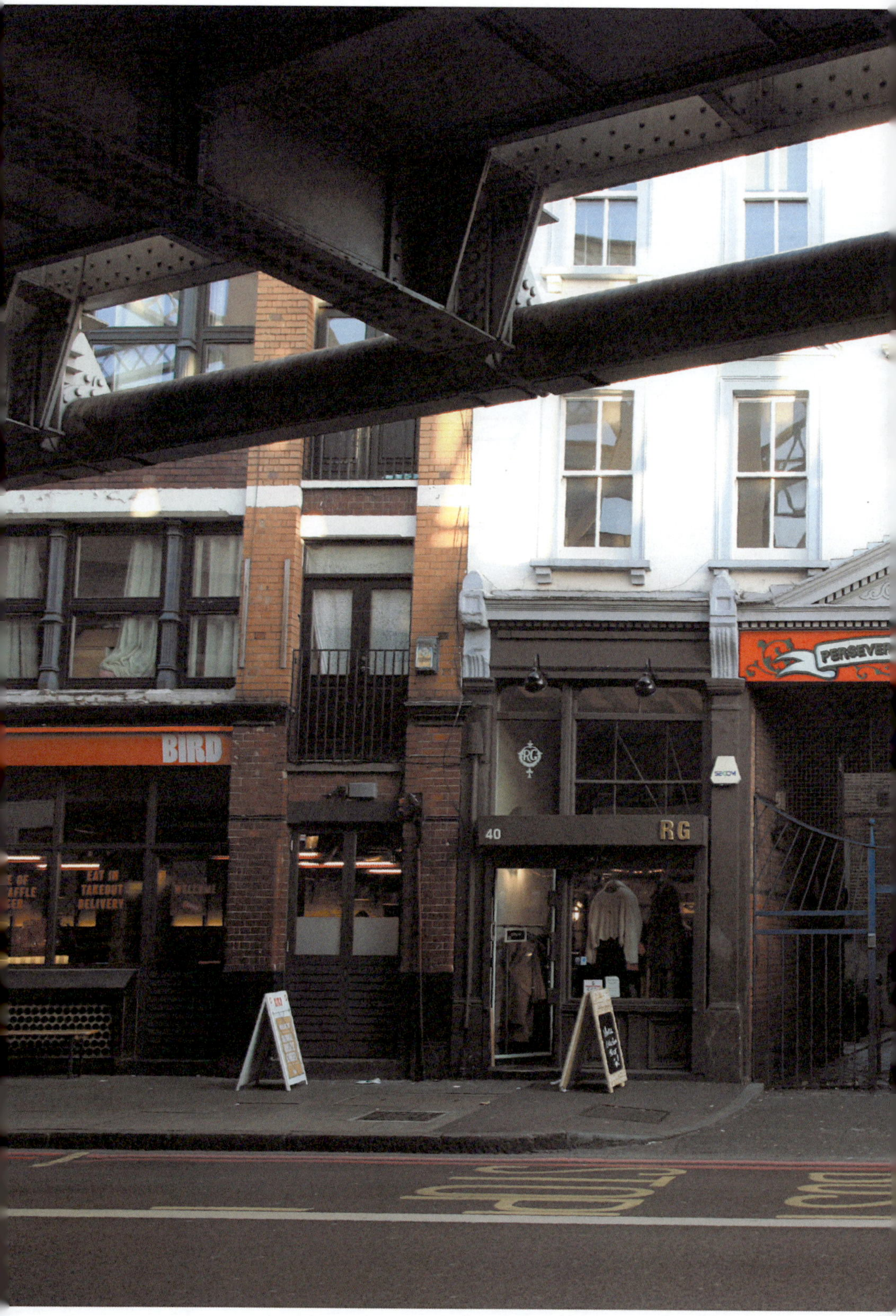
BIRD
EAT IN
TAKEOUT
DELIVERY
40
RG
PERSEVER

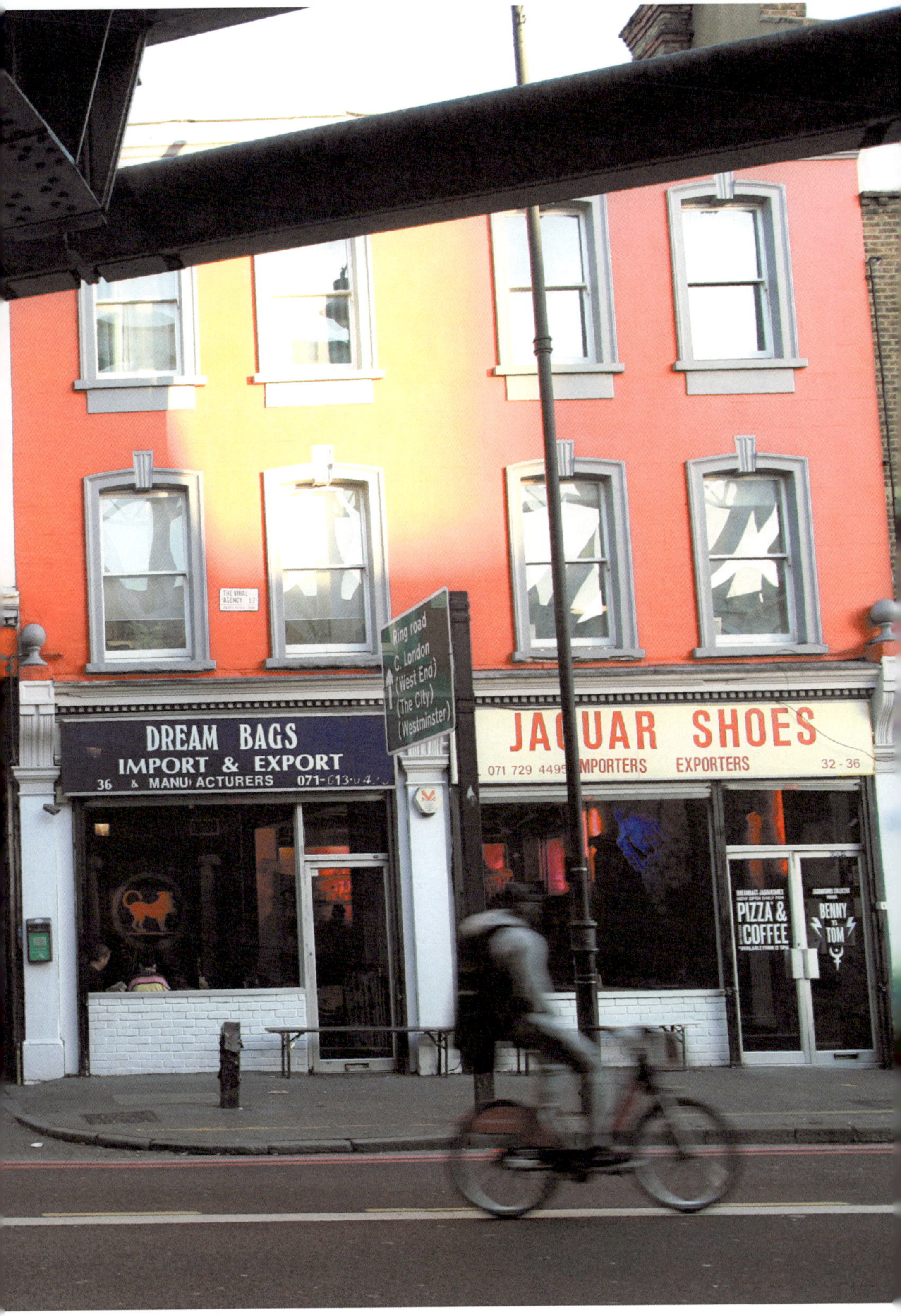
DREAM BAGS
IMPORT & EXPORT
36
SHOES
071 729 4495
EXPORTERS
32 - 36
Ring road
C. London
(West End)
(The City)
(Westminster)
PIZZA &
COFFEE
BENNY
TOM

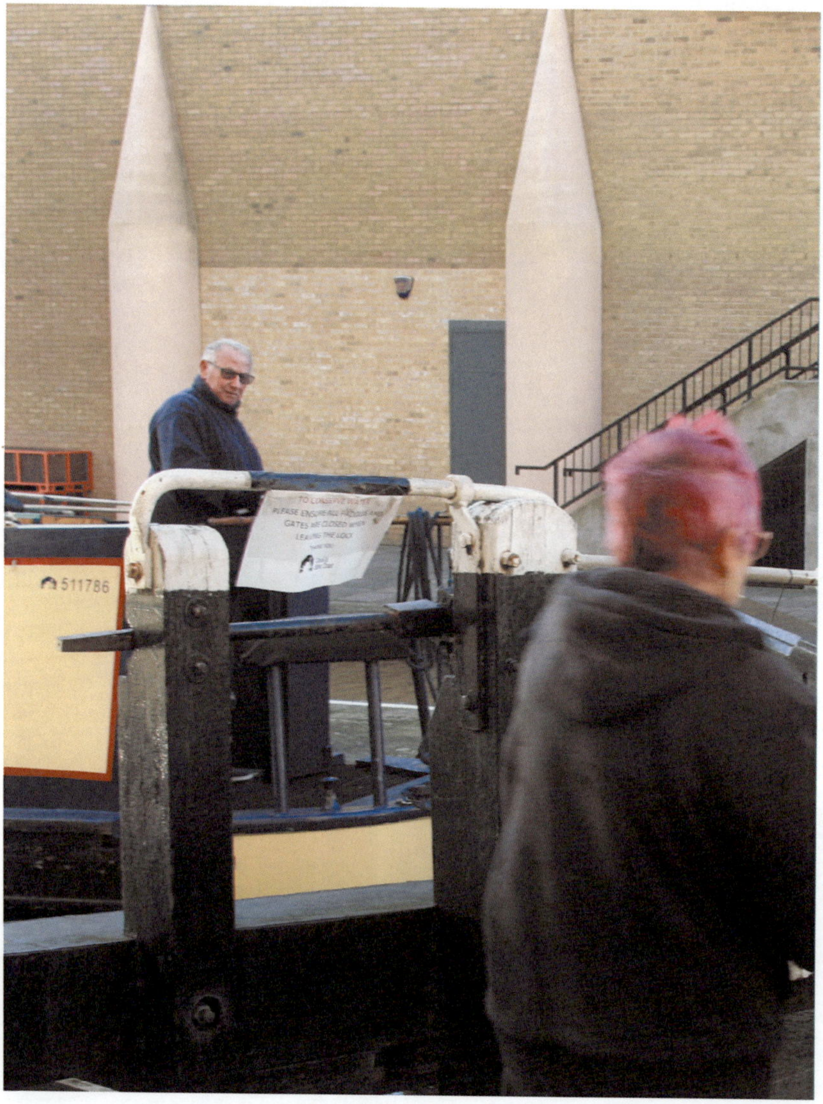
511786

THE REASON BEHIND THE RHYME

Edmund Spenser, 1552 to 1599, was an infamous English poet and his sense of wit and irony struck a cord with Tudor Queen Elizabeth I. Born in East Smithfield, London, Spenser published his first epic poem, The Faerie Queene, that can be read on several levels of allegory, including his praise for Elizabeth herself. She was so delighted with this intellectual entertainment that she invited Edmund to Court and offered him a life pension of £50 a year for his entertainments.

Hungrily the Queen ordered additional poems. There's a story that the Queen told her Lord High Treasurer, William Cecil, to pay Spenser £100 for an additional – and special – poem for her birthday, an unspeakable amount of money for the 16th Century, when an average labourer earned £2 a year.

The Treasurer not unreasonably fumed at the prospect of handing over such an outrageous wage to a mere poet – to which the Queen replied, *"Then give him what is reason" ("Give him what you imagine is the right amount.")*. *"Nothing"*, thought the Treasurer, Lord Cecil. So, without receiving his due payment, when it was time to recite the newly written poem, Spenser gave the Queen his gratitudes:

I was promis'd on a time,
To have a reason for my rhyme,
From that time unto this season,
I receiv'd nor rhyme nor reason.

The Queen immediately ordered her Treasurer to pay Spenser the original £100.

This fuelled the beginning of Sarcasm, first recorded in Smithfield in 1579, with Spenser's annotation to 'The Shepheardes Calender':

"Tom piper, an ironicall Sarcasmus, spoken in derision of these rude wits, whych..."

TUDOR SARCASM : *A MAN WITH A BIG NOSE*

But it was the Spanish court that fanned the flames of sarcasm with two feuding poets. Francisco de Quevedo y Villages, amused gentry in the Courts of Madrid of 1645, with this to say about his rival poet, Don Luis de Góngora y Argote...

A man to a nose was glued,
Once it was an unsurpassable nose,
A gown-sized nose that's hunched like a scribe,
A mean swordfish with protruding nasal pubes.
It was a sundial that is badly faced,
It was thoughtful distilling vessel
An upside down elephant above the mouth,
The grandest nose from Ovid Nason.
The pointing end of the Galley's prow,
Once it was a Pyramid of Egypt,
The twelve tribes of noses was.
The owner of the infinite nose so fierce
That in the face of High Priest Annas it was a crime.

Don Luis returned the insult to his rival, Quevedo, announcing:

Mr Anacreon, no one can stumble upon you,
That does not say with much courtesy,
Since your feet are a sad poem,
And your lightness is like grape syrup.
Will not you imitate the comedies of Lope,
That everyday Bellerophon does wear comic poetry clogs
and puts on his spurs, to give Pegasus a gallop?
With special care your spectacles want to translate into Greek,
Not having looked by your eyes.
I lend my puckered brown eye a little time to the spectacles,
Because I revealed some loose verses
So all you will understand is about the pantaloons.

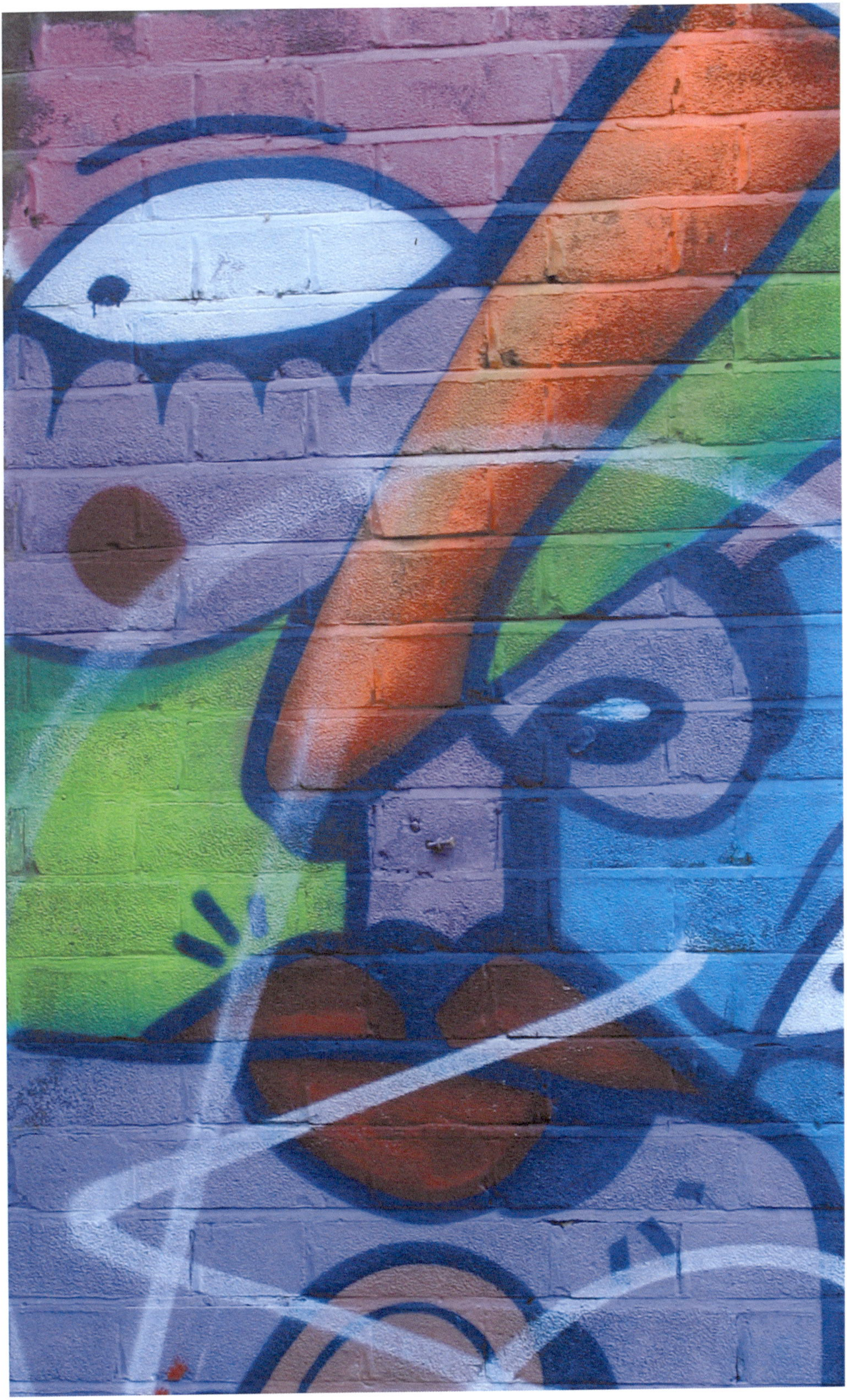

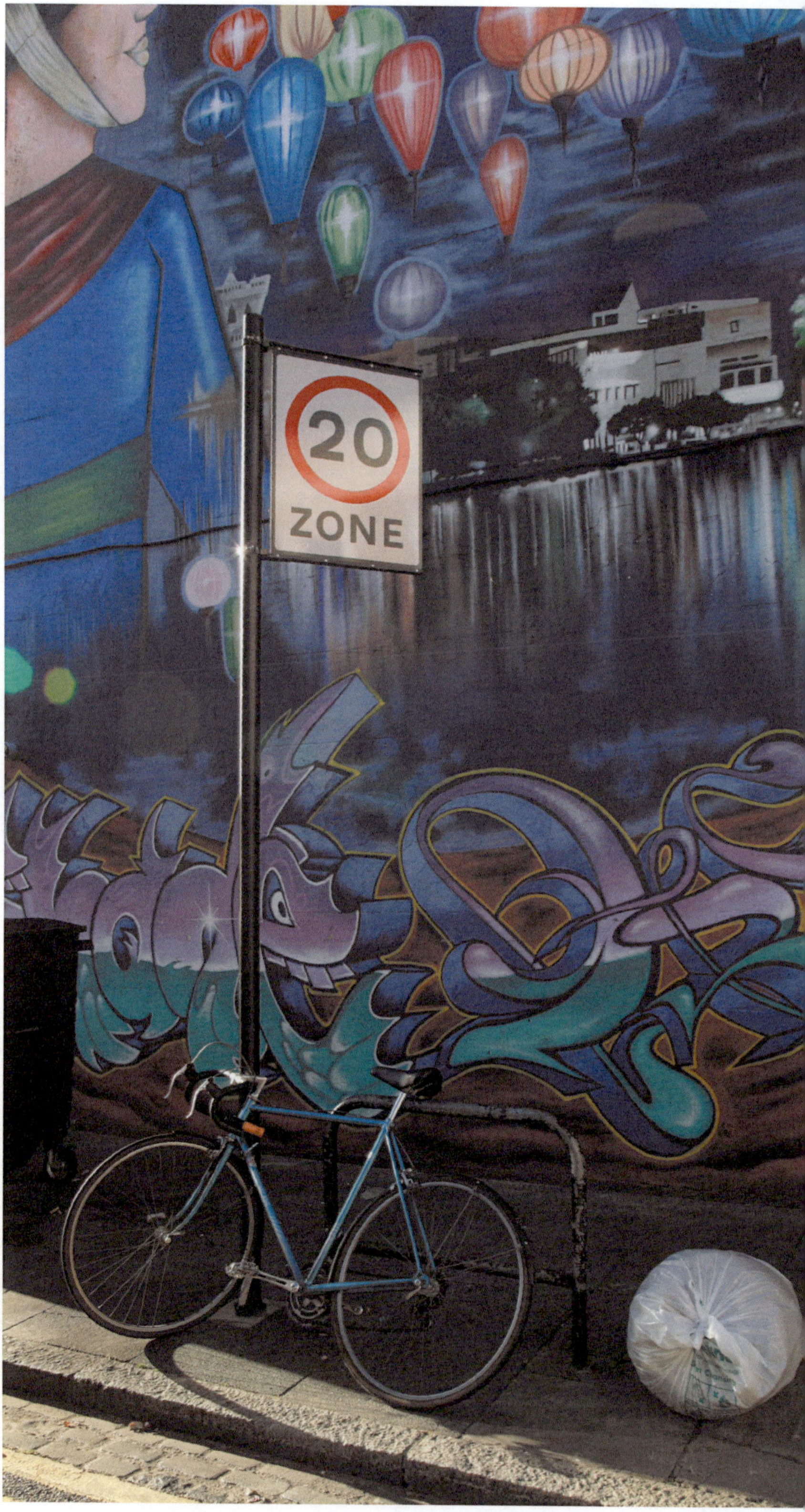
20
ZONE

HOW PURPLE WAS INVENTED IN SHADWELL

Chemist William Perkin wanted to cure malaria. Instead, he started a new movement in the fashion industry.

In 1856, Perkin was an 18-year-old student at the Royal College of Chemistry. He attempted to create artificial quinine, an anti-malaria drug derived from tree bark. He was unsuccessful. However, his curiosity was piqued when his failures resulted in a thick, purple sludge.

The colour caught his eye. The sludge, made with a carbon-rich tar from distilled coal, took on a unique shade of purple, a very popular colour in the fashion world at the time. Perkin was able to isolate the compound producing the colour, which he named *"Mauve"*. Perkin had created the first-ever synthetic dye.

Perkin dropped out of school and his father, George, used his entire life savings to build a factory that produced mauve-coloured items. Within a few years, the family became extremely wealthy. Perkin's dye was quite vibrant and didn't fade or wash out, but that's not the only good thing that came from Perkin's new colour. Mauve helped kick-start a chemistry revolution. Experiments from other labs soon resulted in thousands of useful carbon compounds, such as an actual artificial quinine.

Shadwell lies at the end of a rainbow. In 1856 it transcended its dank and slimy sounding name with the birth of a dazzling colour. Aniline dyes, invented just off Cable Street, stormed on to the market, brightening clothes and homes as never before.

COULD IT HAVE BECOME PERKIN'S PURPLE?

William Perkin's dye was a profoundly patrician purple. He sent a sample of purple cloth to a Scots dyer and it aroused cautious interest. It was valuable but would it cost too much? It did not. Perkin abandoned his pure science career in its cradle and, with money stumped up by his father, started manufacturing his dye. He had to become an expert in dying first, because the colour was initially not as 'fast' as he hoped and he had to find a way to make it stick – and then because he needed to nudge the methods of his industrial customers from their folkloric origins towards the scientific.

In 1858 he opened his colour factory, appropriately, in Greenford. Greenford now has the William Perkin High School and its uniform, we are pleased to report, is purple.

At this point Perkin had another stroke of luck. Purple had come into fashion. The Empress Eugénie was wearing purple in 1857, and everyone wanted it. Once, only Roman emperors wore purple, extracted from sea snails in the Near East. In fact purple was so exclusive that for centuries our own noble Lords had to make do with crimson. Now though, Perkin could turn dirt into dye.

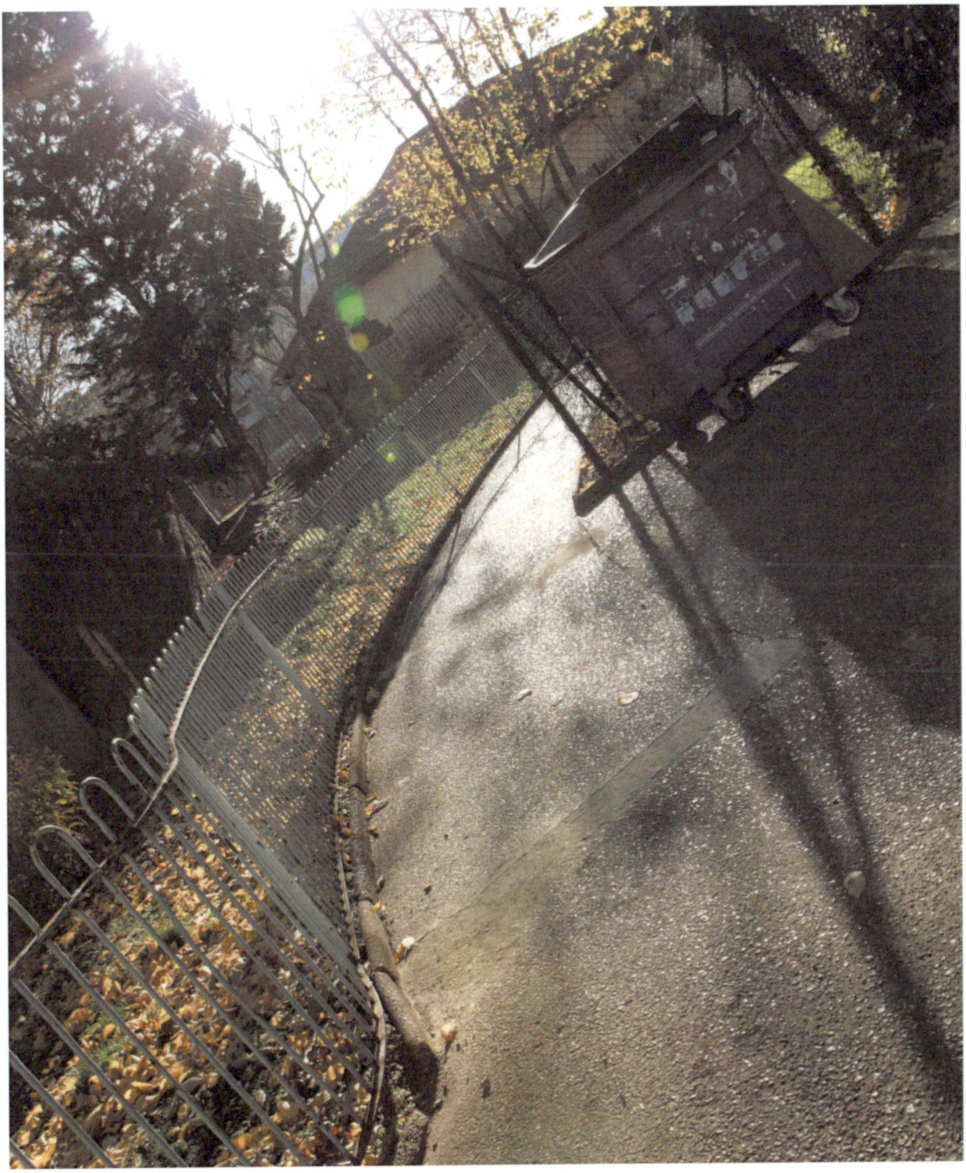

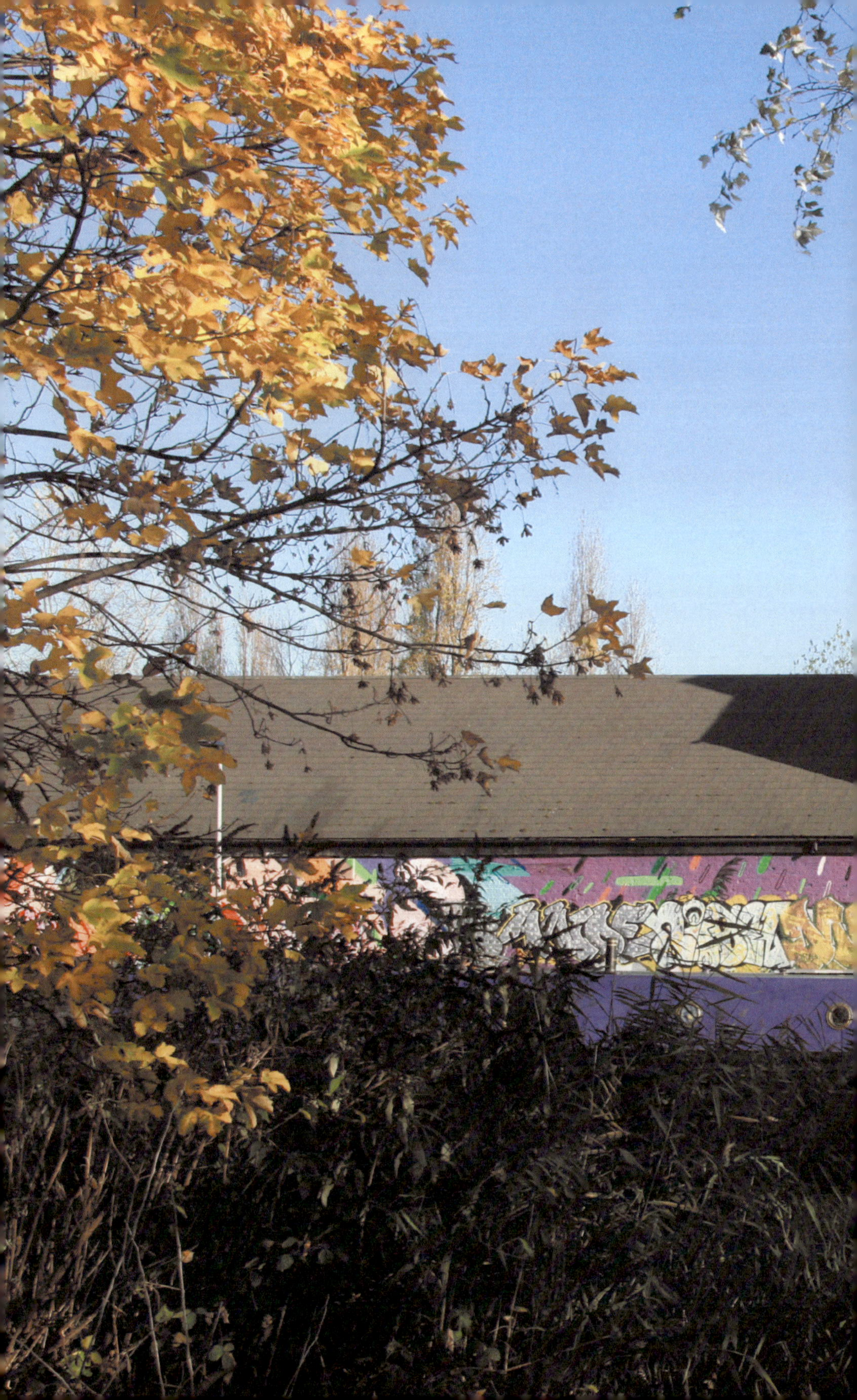

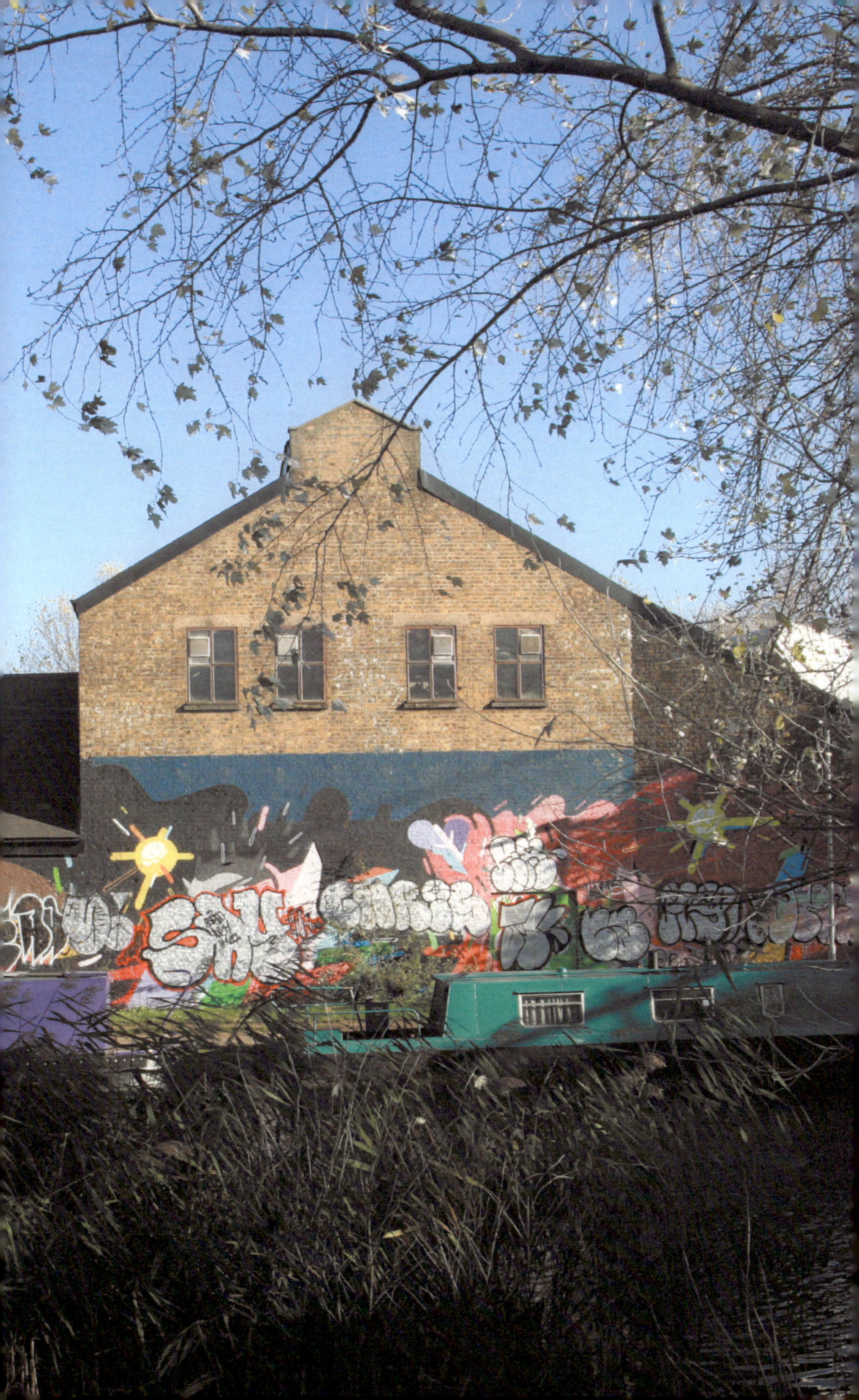

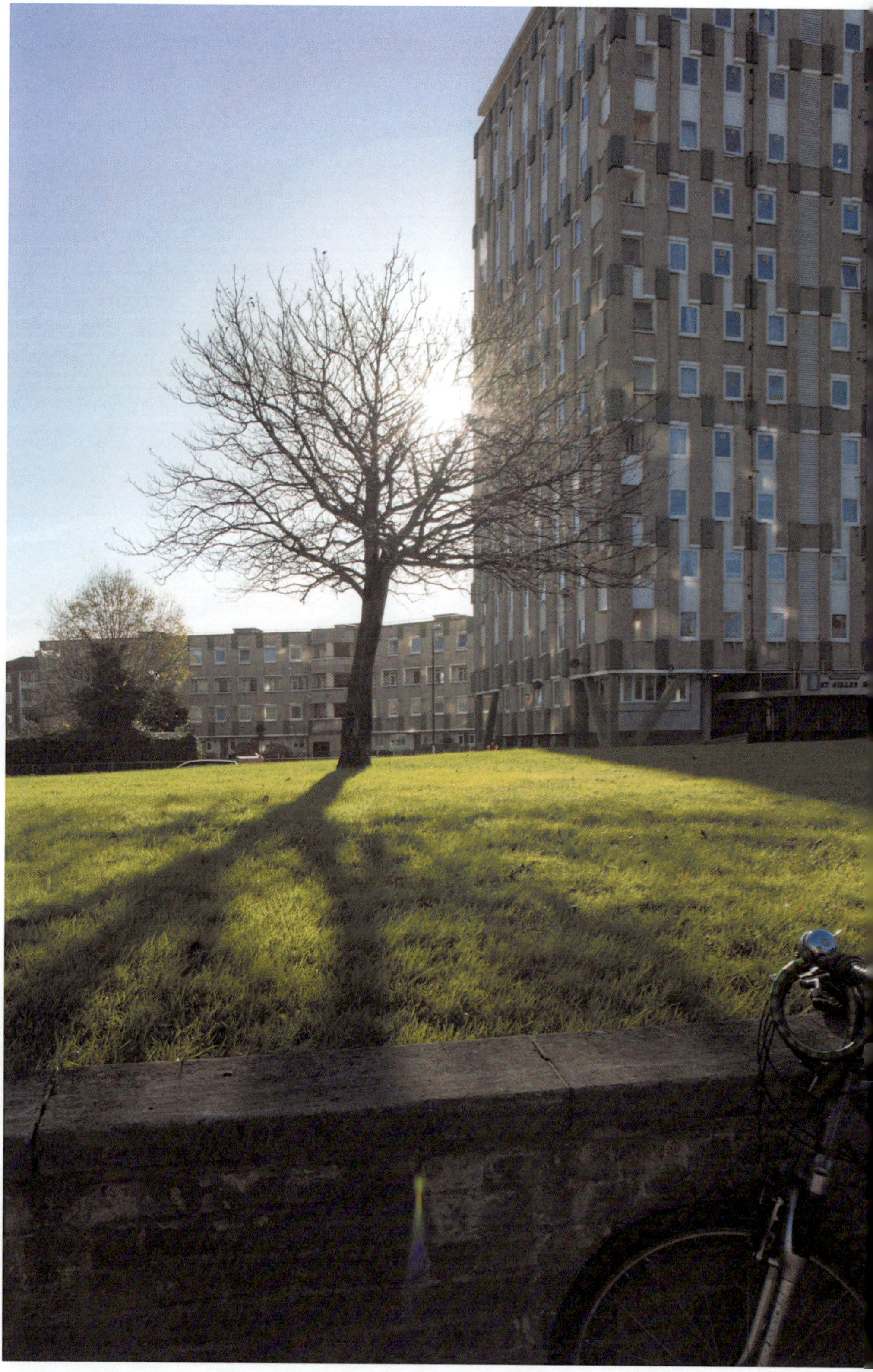

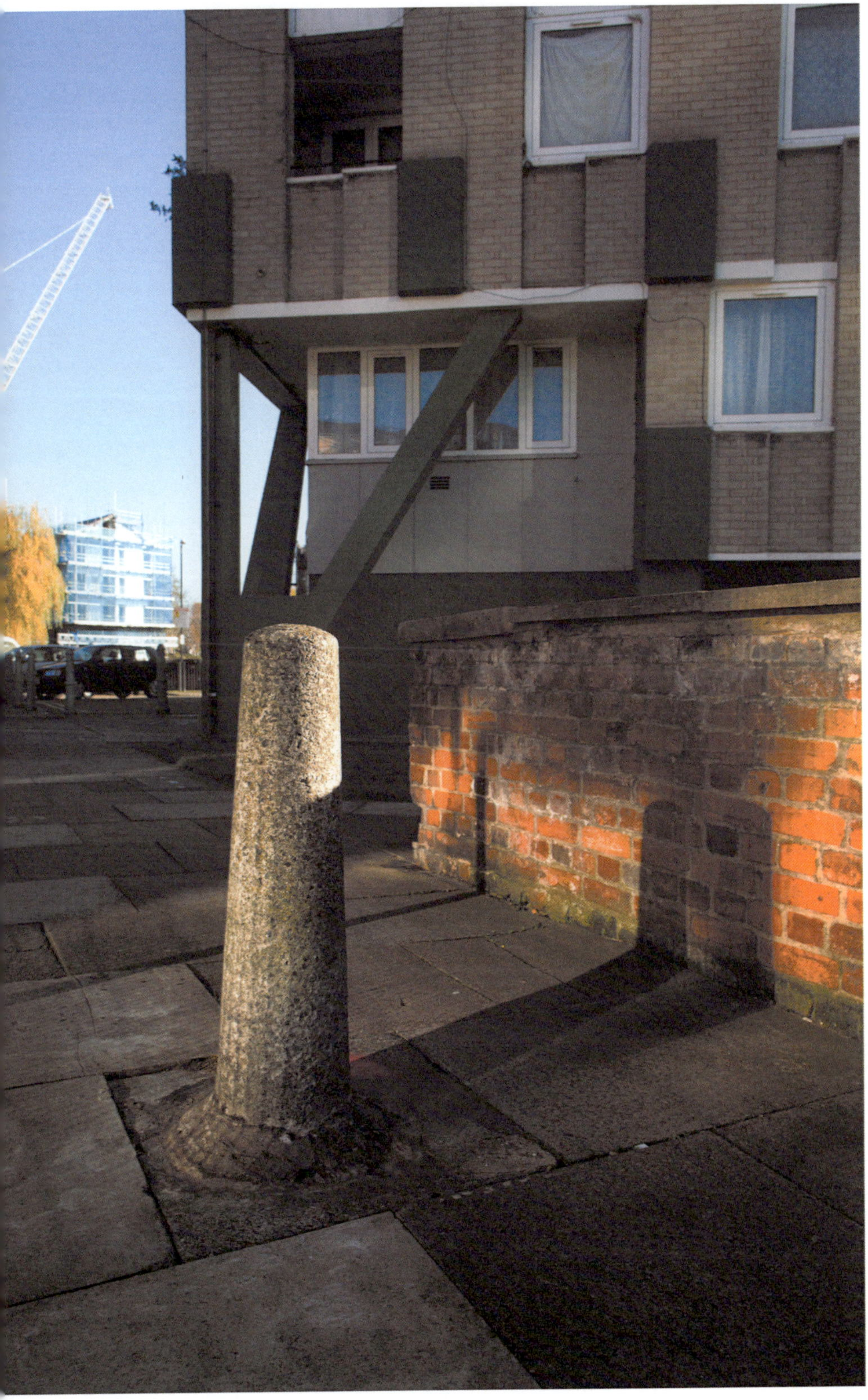

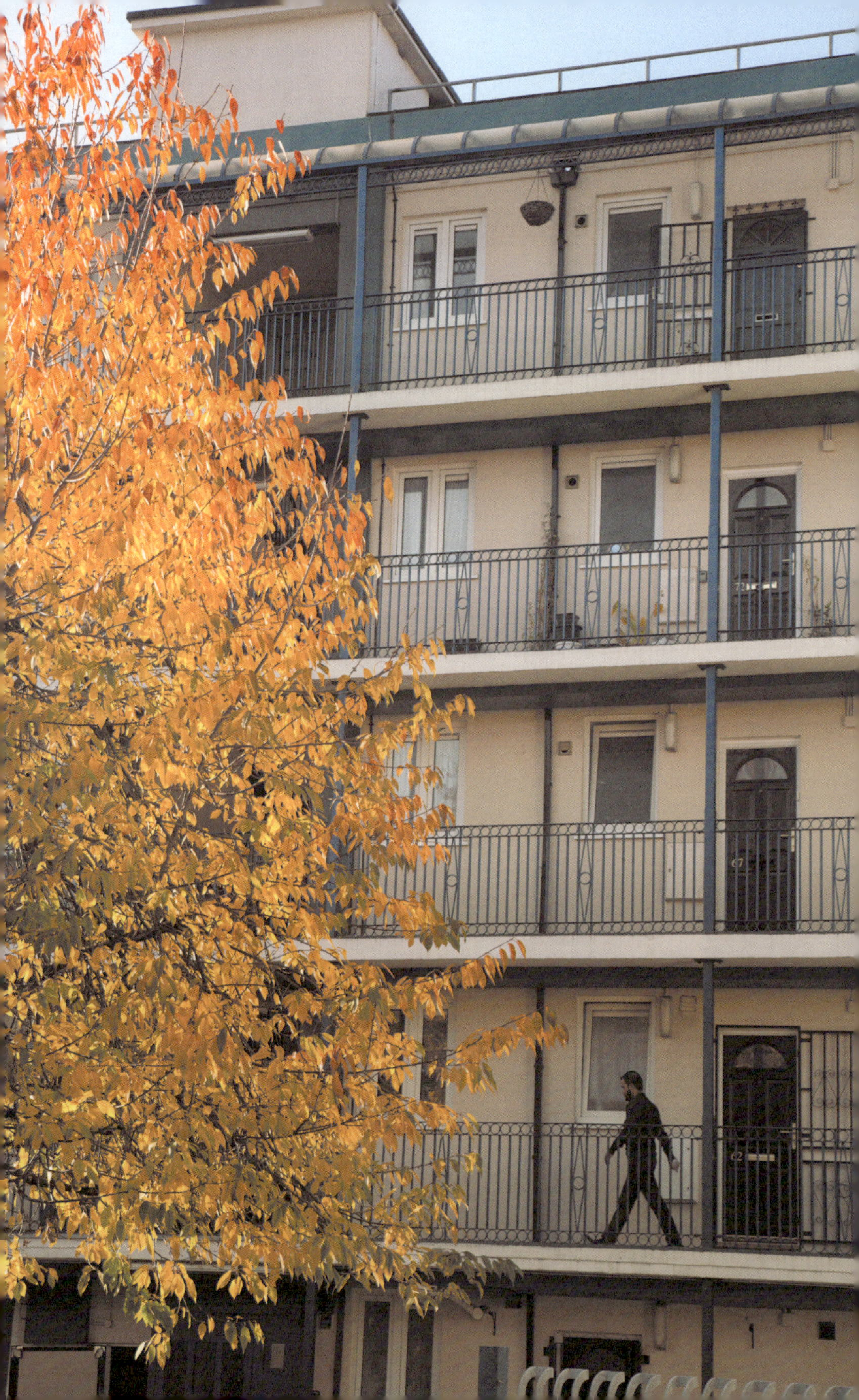

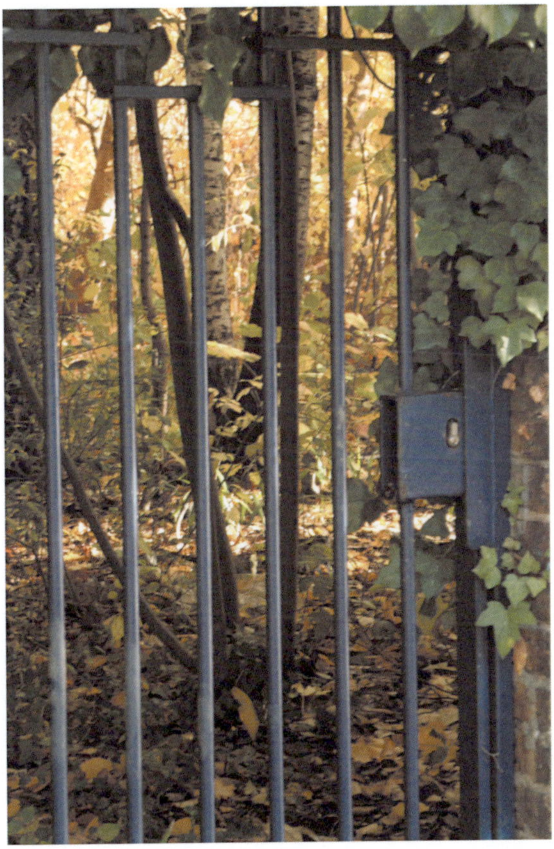

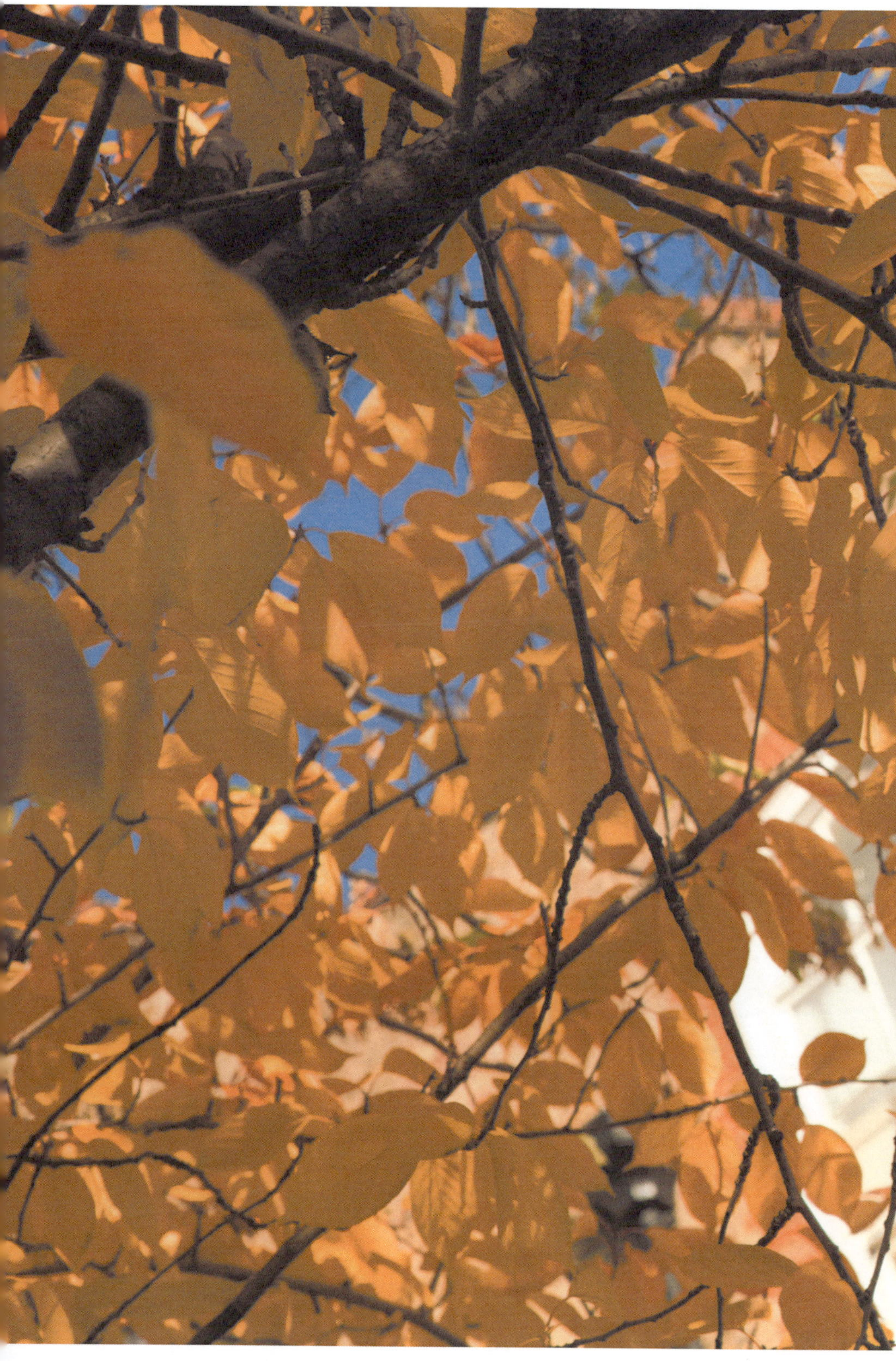

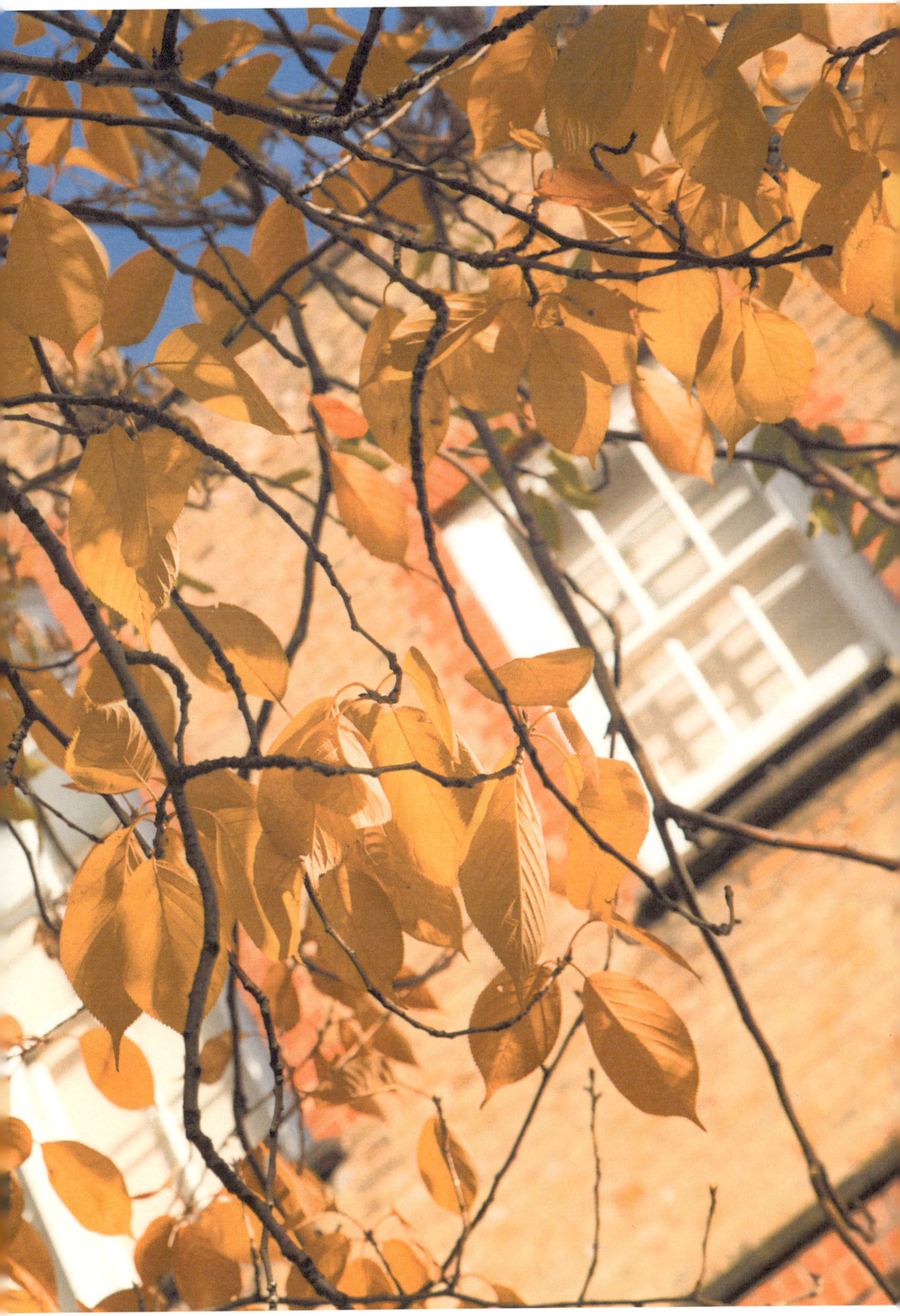

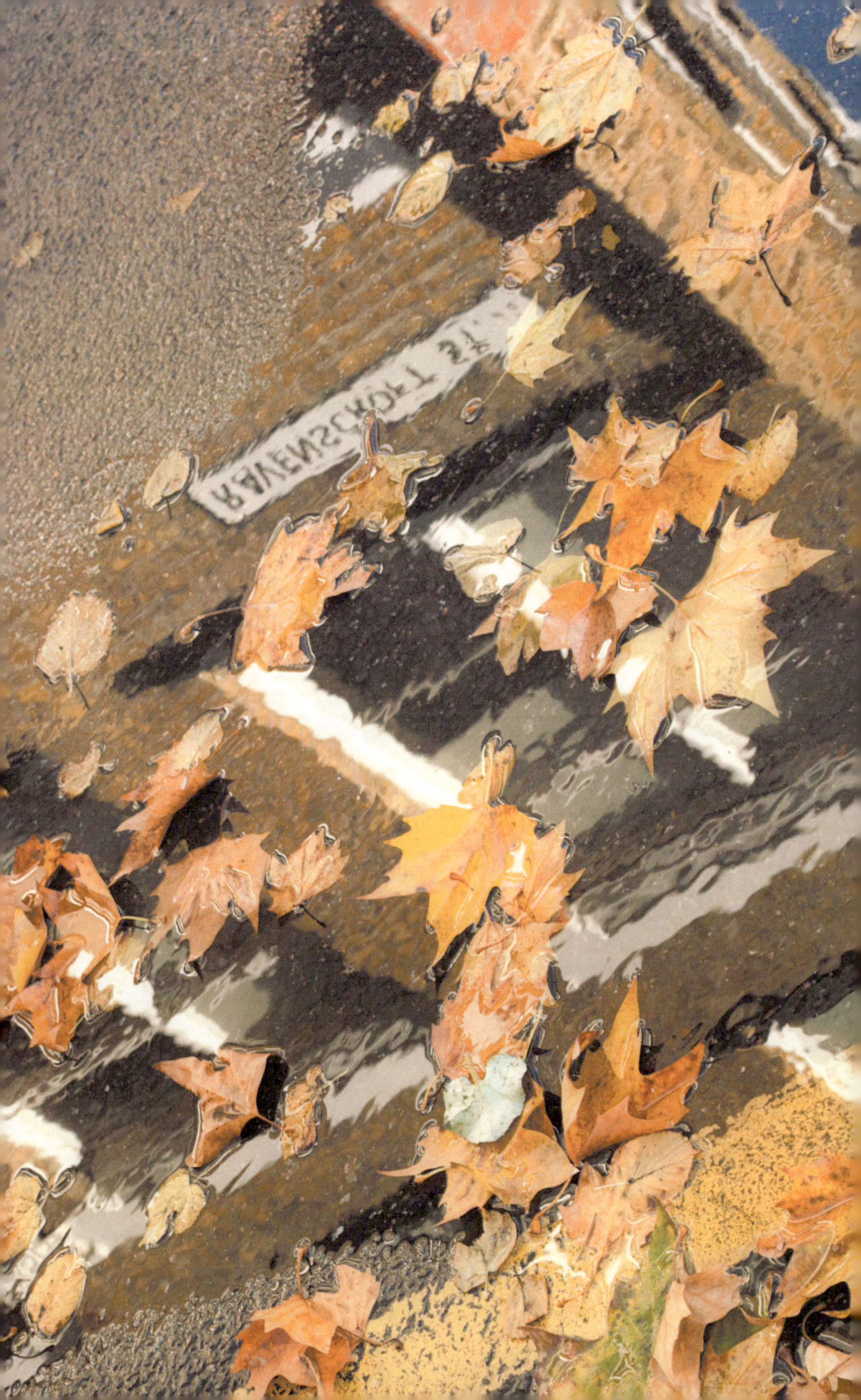
RAVENSCROFT ST

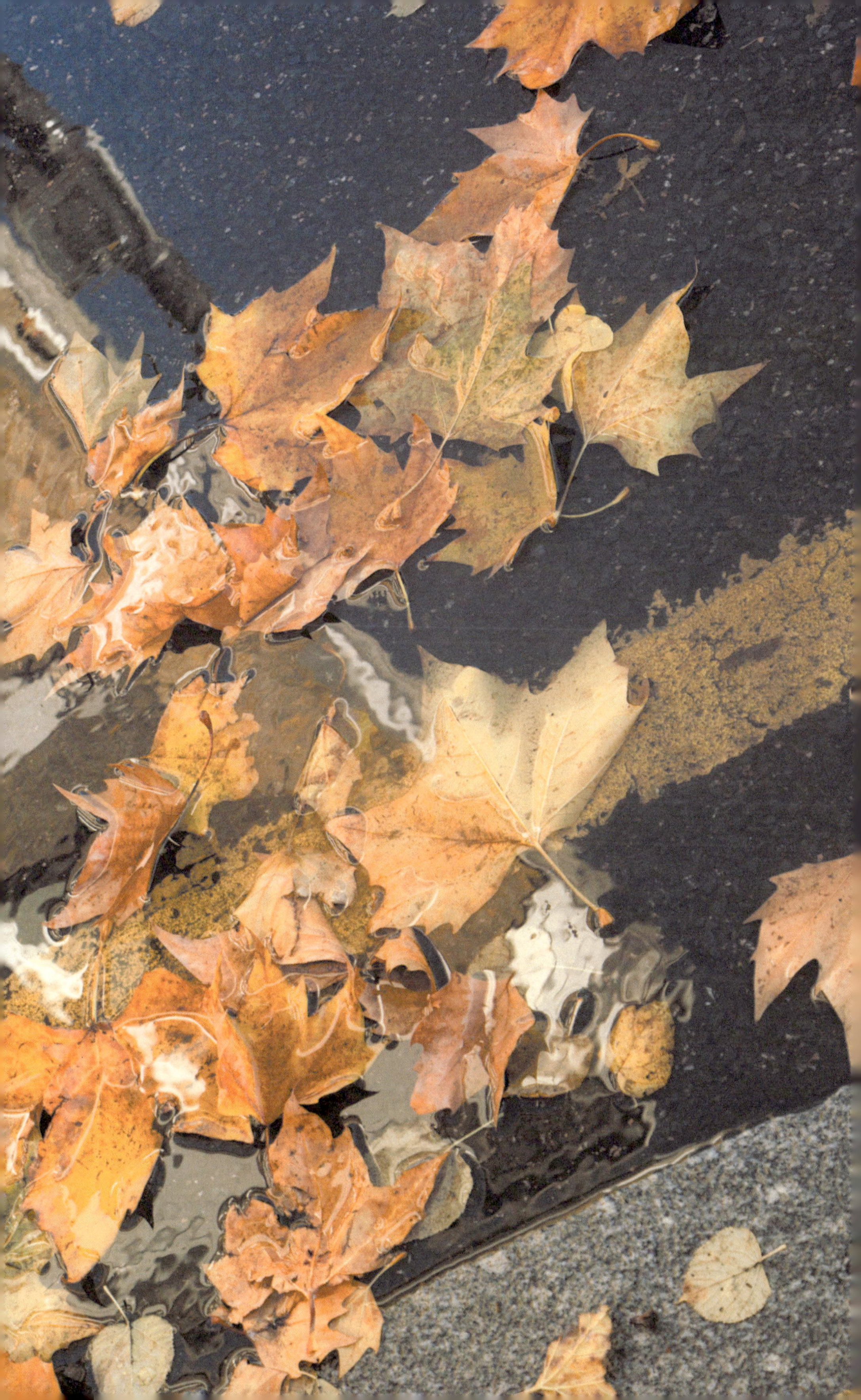

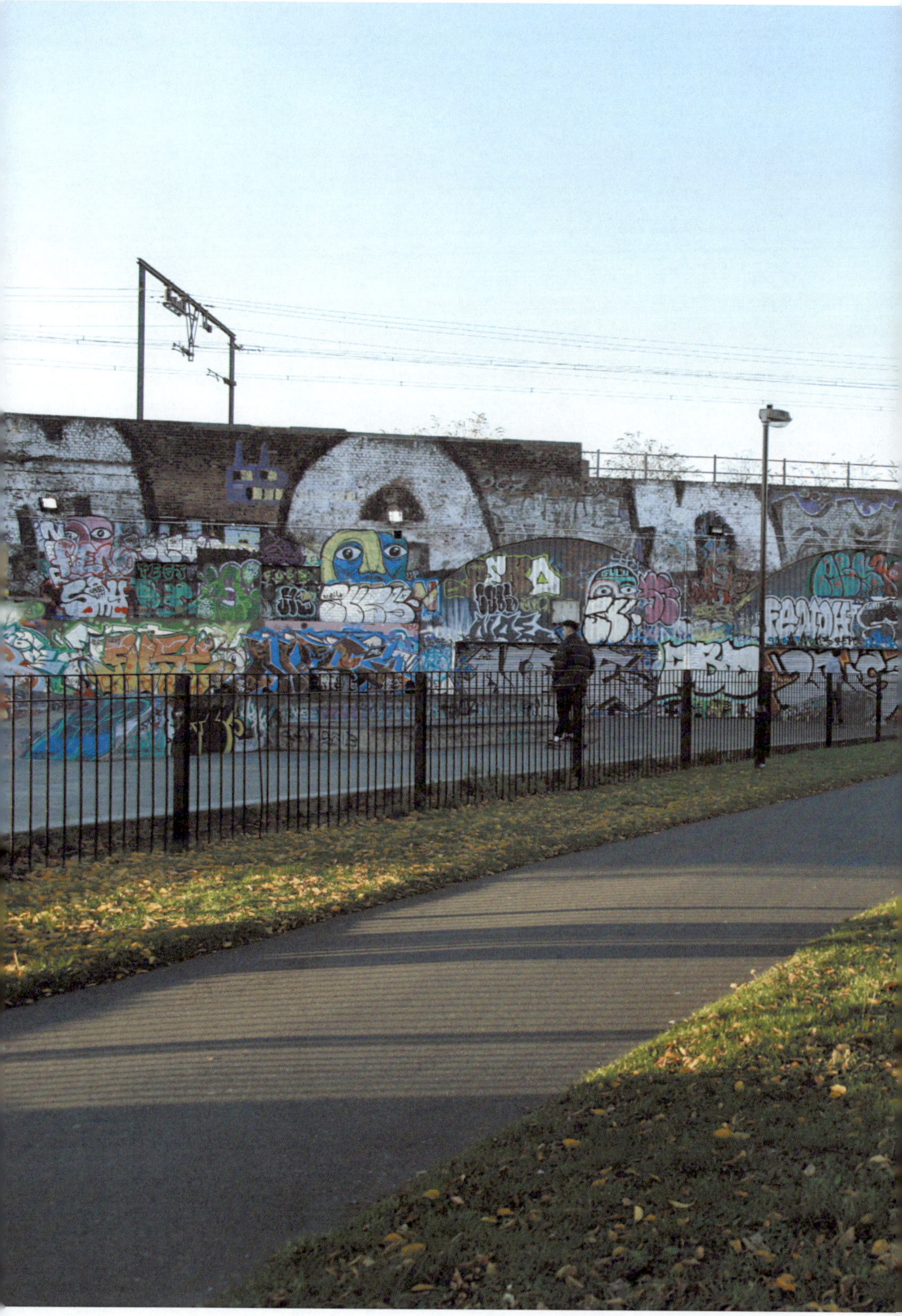

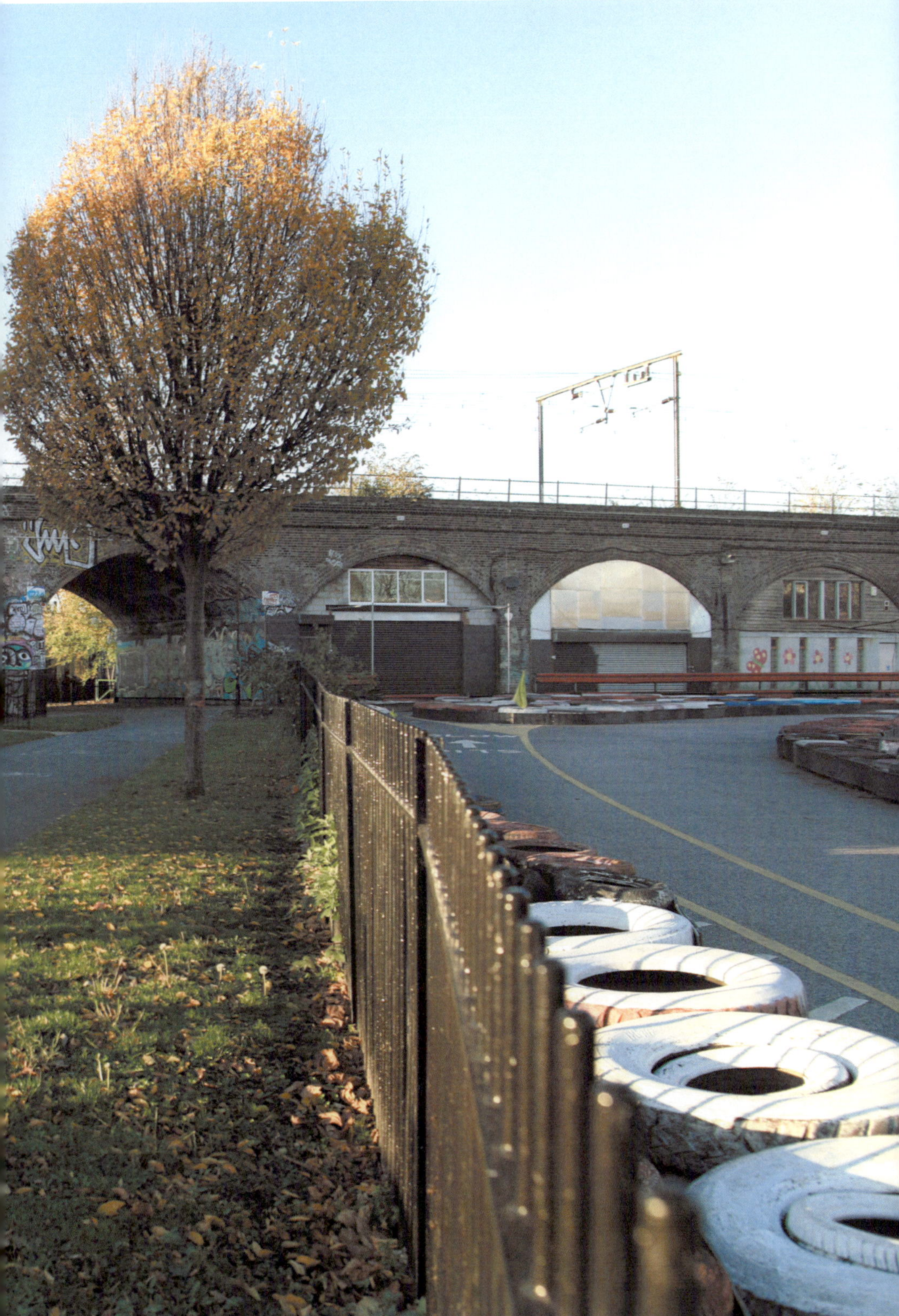

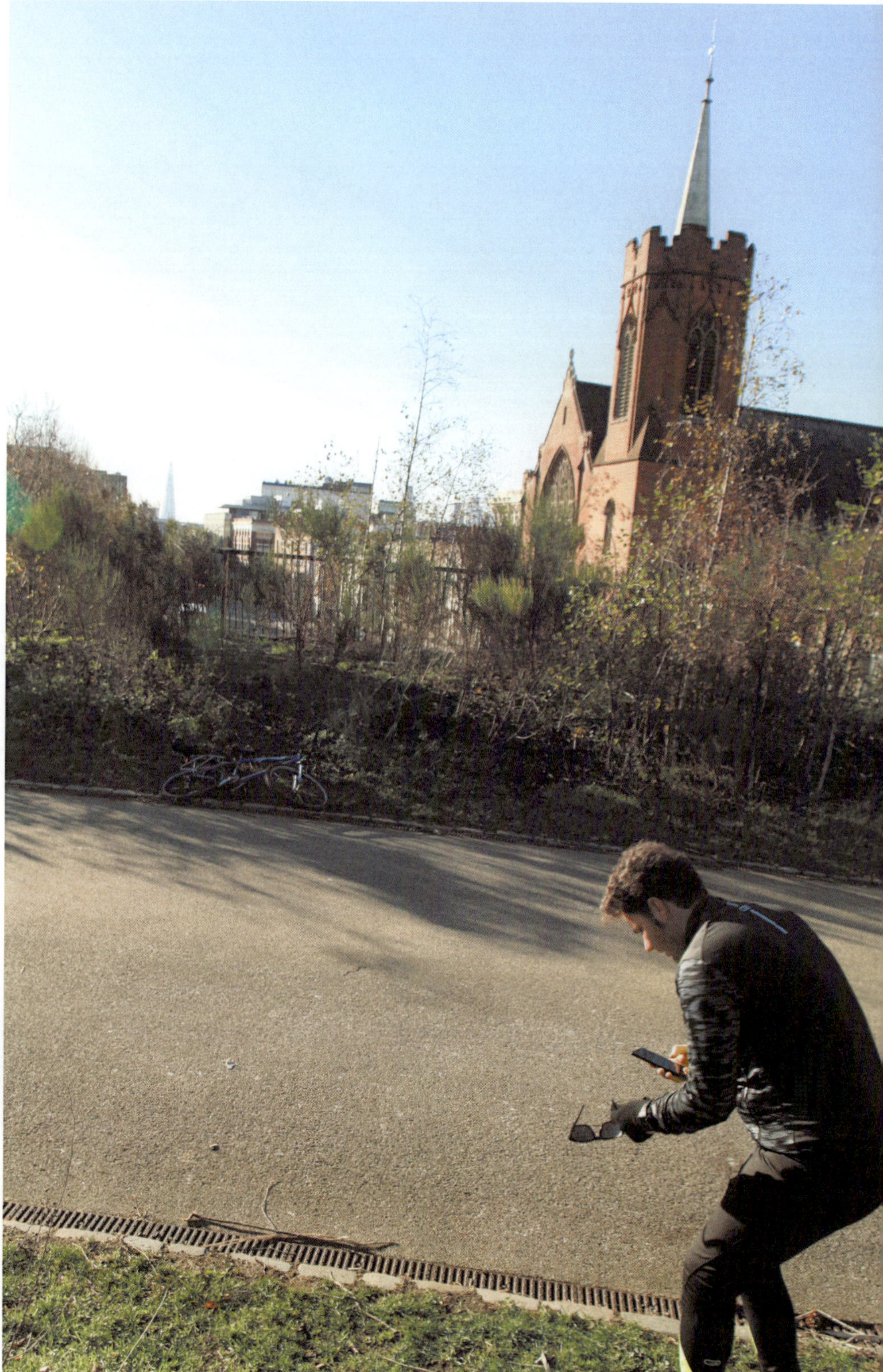

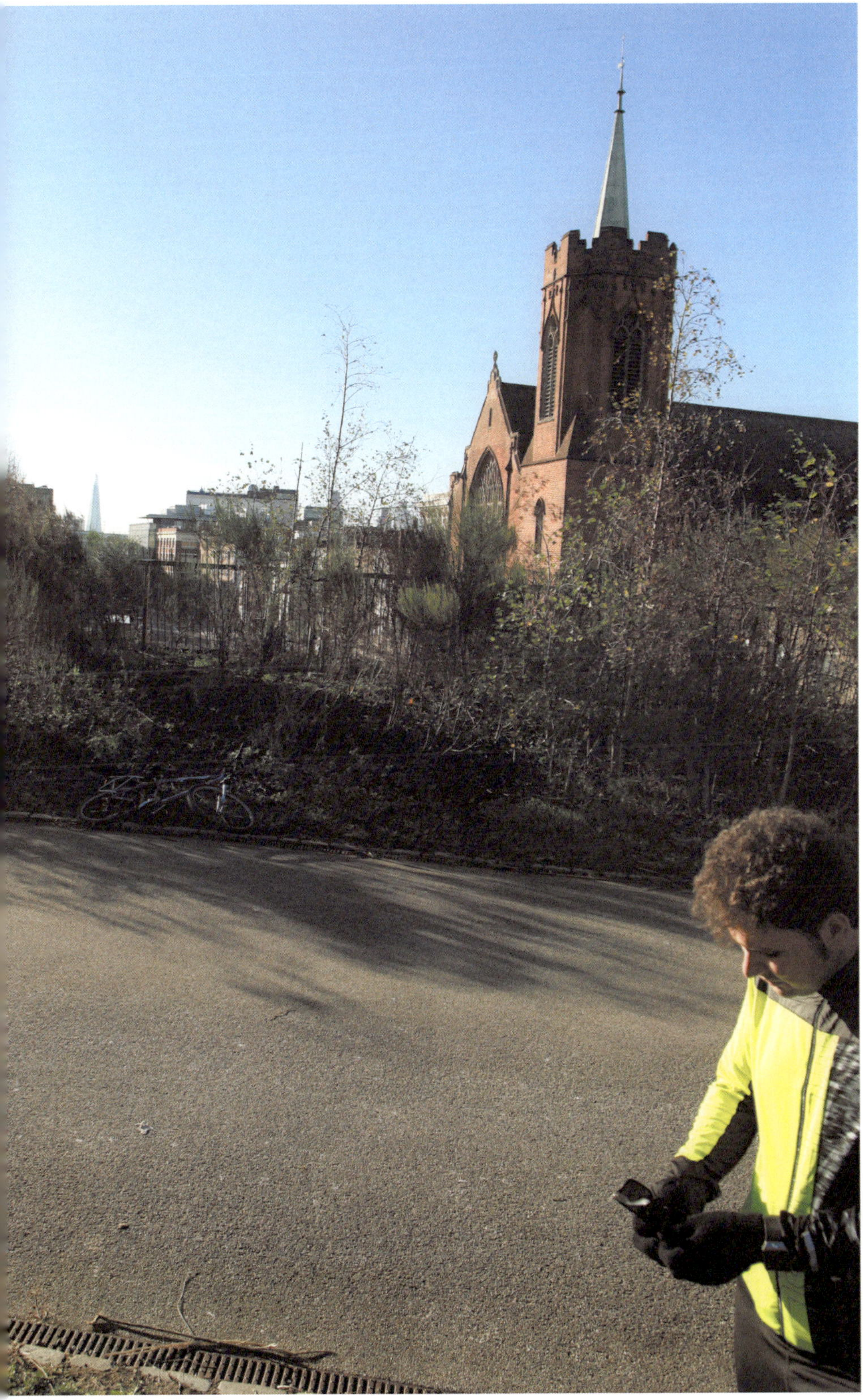

MILE END WONDERS

Once a toll road – whose mile was judged by markers between the Black Boy 'Whitechappell' and 'Stepenheth' church – was abolished in 1864 by the Metropolitan Turnpike Act because the tolls were losing business to the rapidly expanding rail network.

But Mile End has a more intriguing secret. Back in the depths of time, a group of citizen longbow men originally trained as the Fraternity of Prince Arthur's Knights. Keen to maintain their employable skills, they practised in the fields and woods near Mile-End and on Mile-End Green. News of this highly talented group reached King Henry VIII who came to see for himself. Impressed by these longbow men and their feastings after major hunting shoots, the King took them under his patronage giving them the Charter known as the Order of Knights of Prince Arthur's Round Table – *"The Unitie Laudable and Fraternitie of Prince Arthur's Knights 1502"*.

Some of the archers were invited to shoot before the King at Windsor, but the East Londoners proved to be the most accurate and impressive archers of all. A string of consecutive titles followed. One such particularly accurate marksmen was given the courtesy title of *"Duke of Shoreditch"*, where he resided. Later other titles followed such as the *"Marquis of Clerkenwell, Islington and Shacklewell"* after where the archers lived.

Shakespeare shot and feasted with the Fraternity and created Falstaff for his plays Henry IV, Part 1 and Part 2, in the second of which, Falstaff, on visits to old Justice Shallow, would reminisce: *"I remember at Mile-End Green, when I lay at Clement's-Inn – I was then Sir Dragonet in Arthur's show"*.

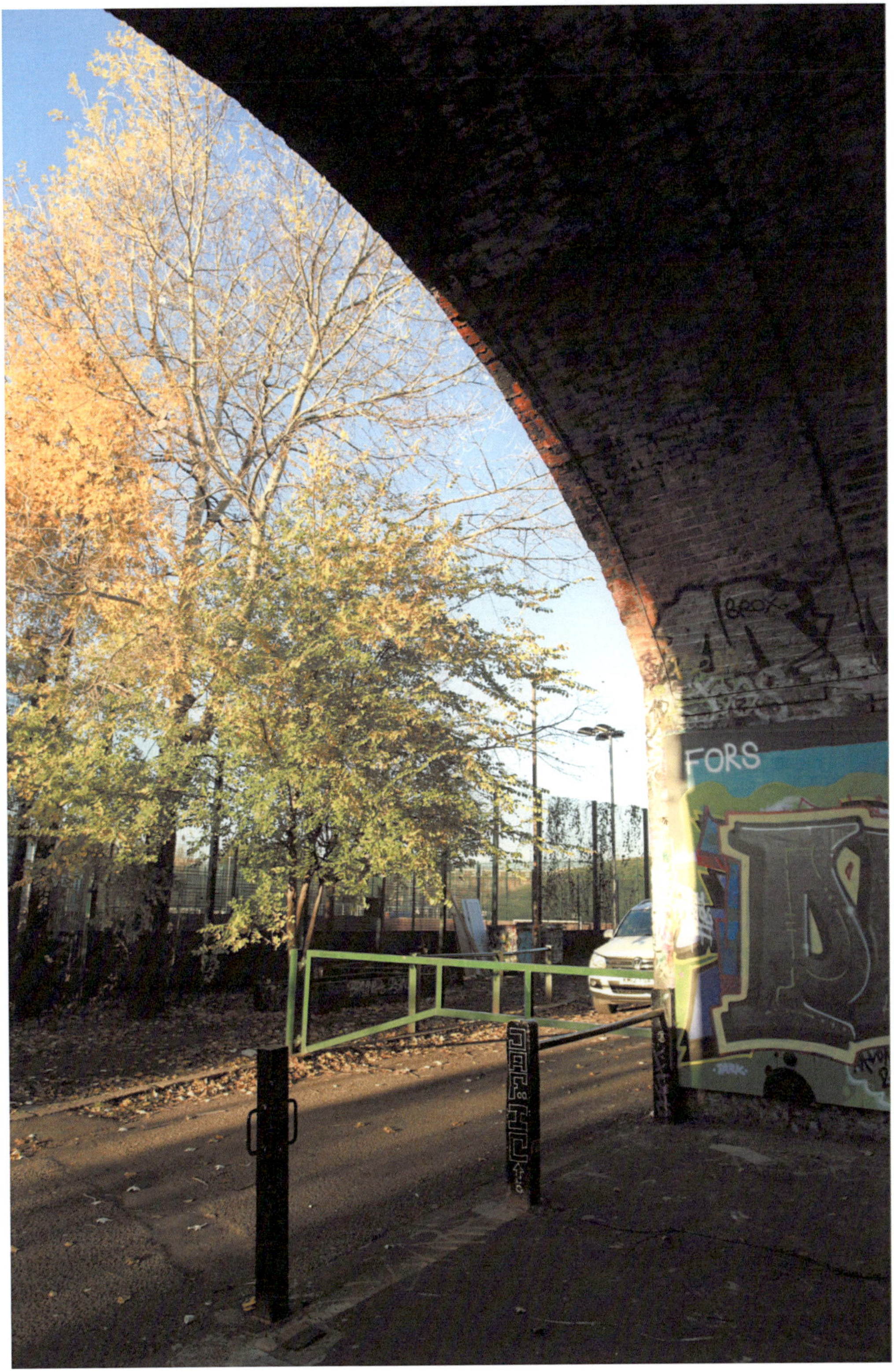
FORS

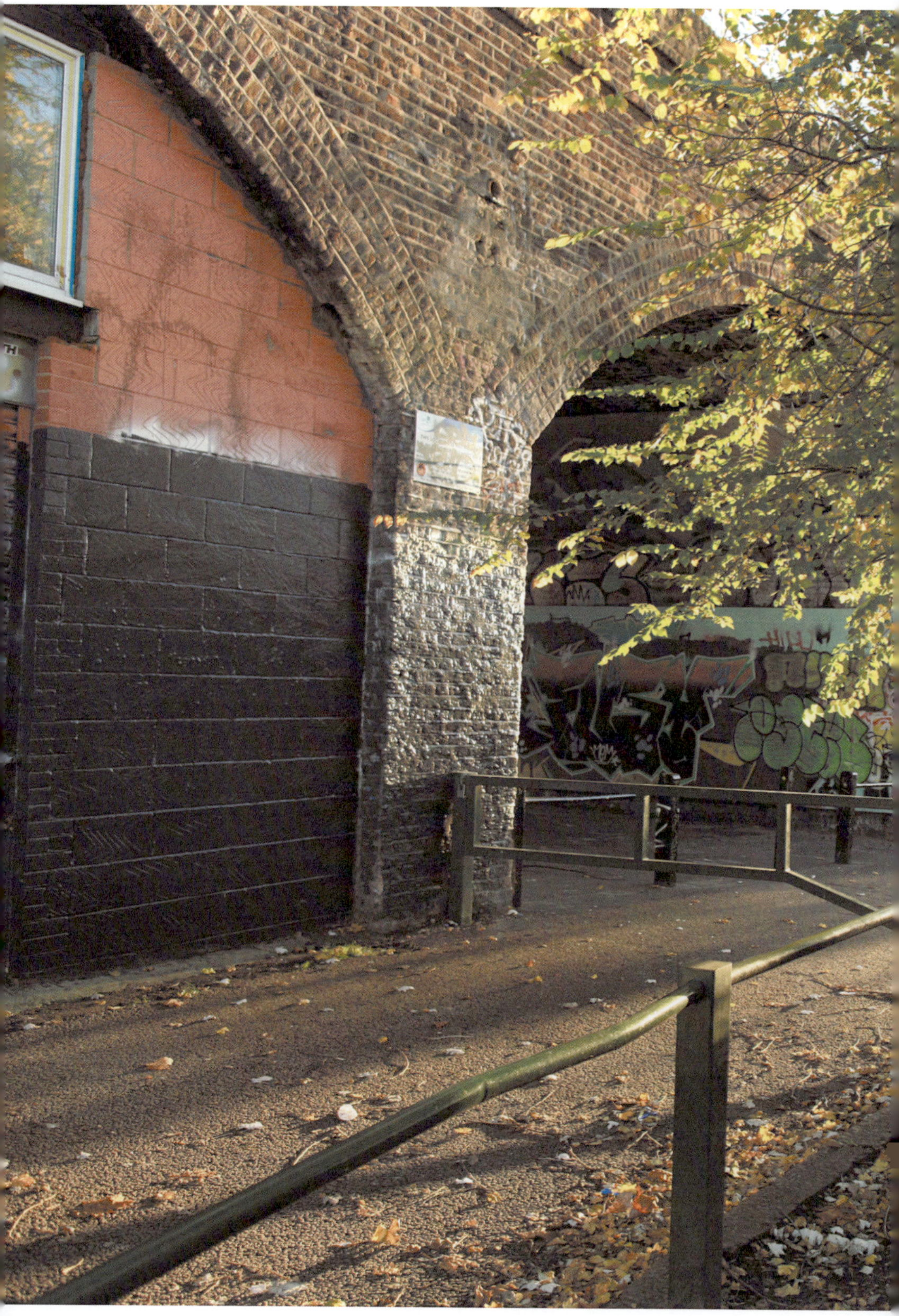

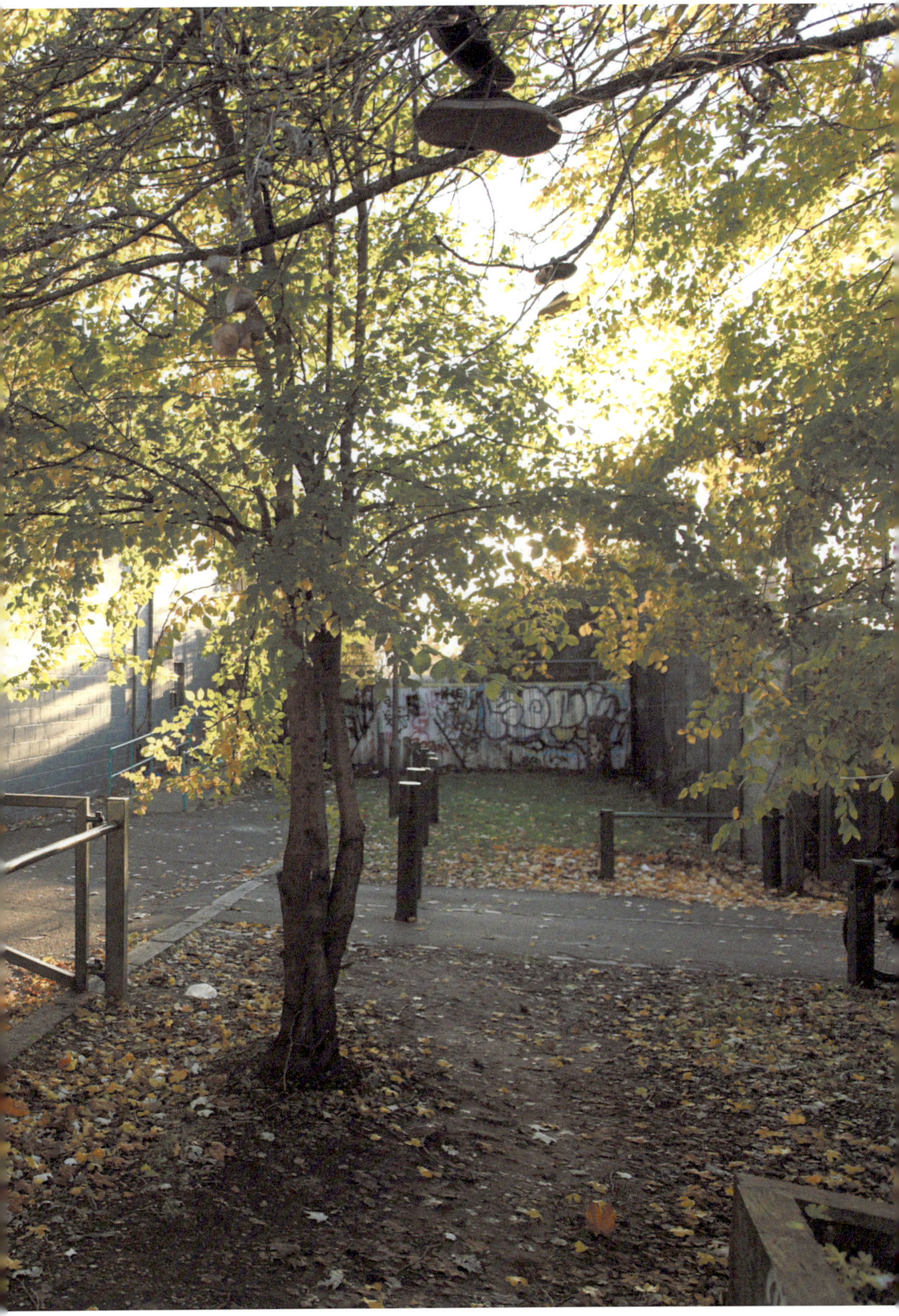

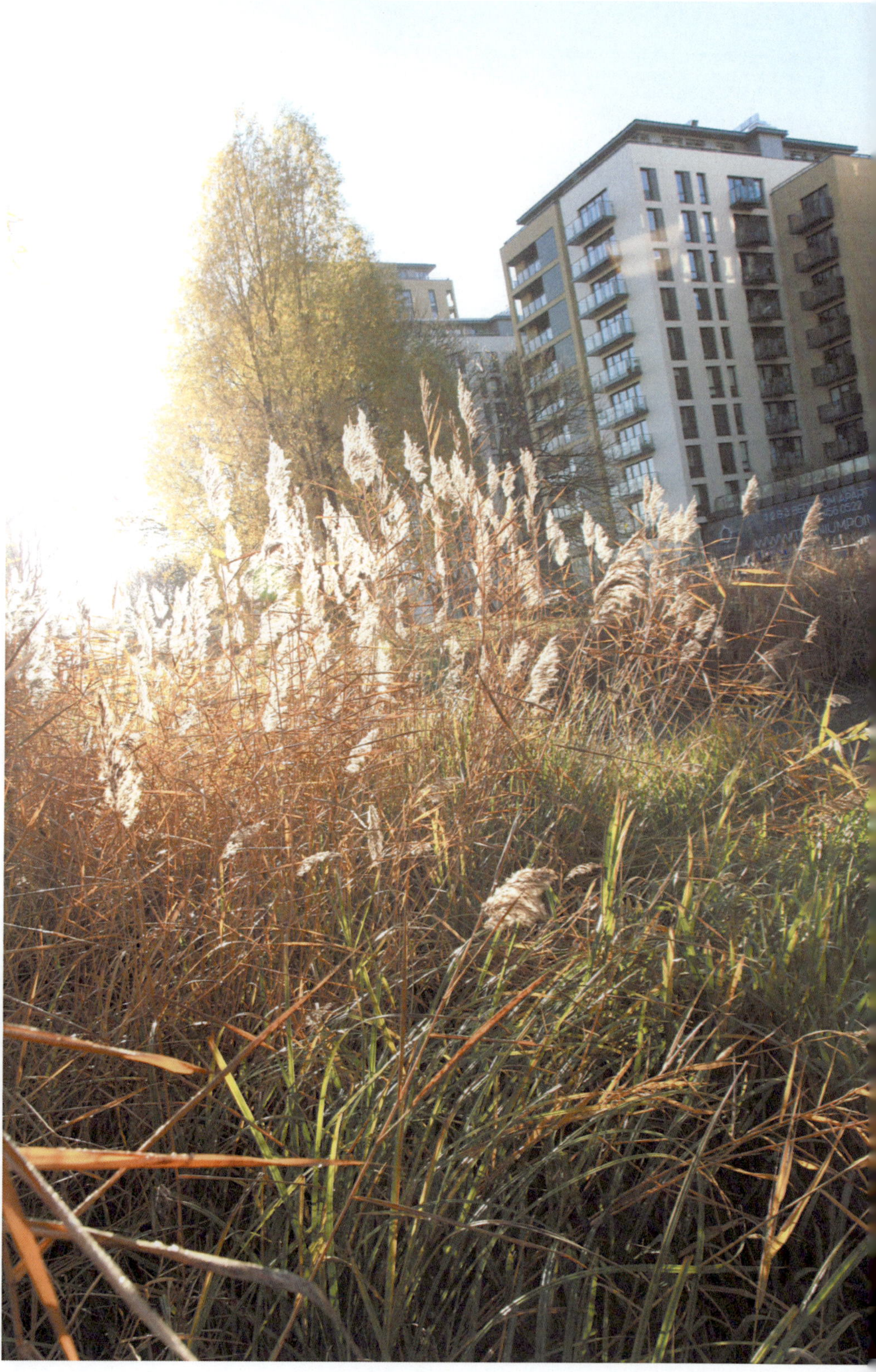

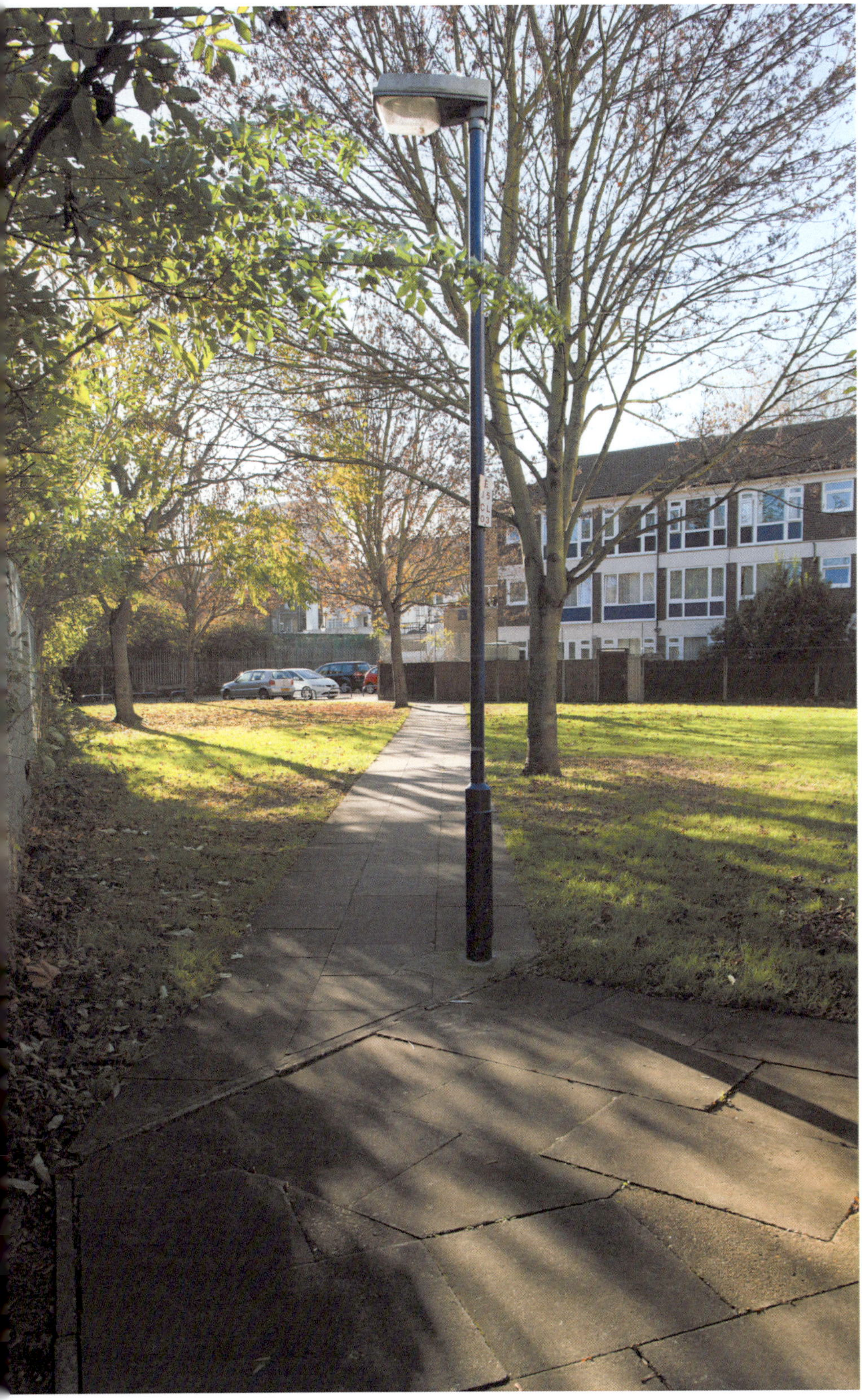

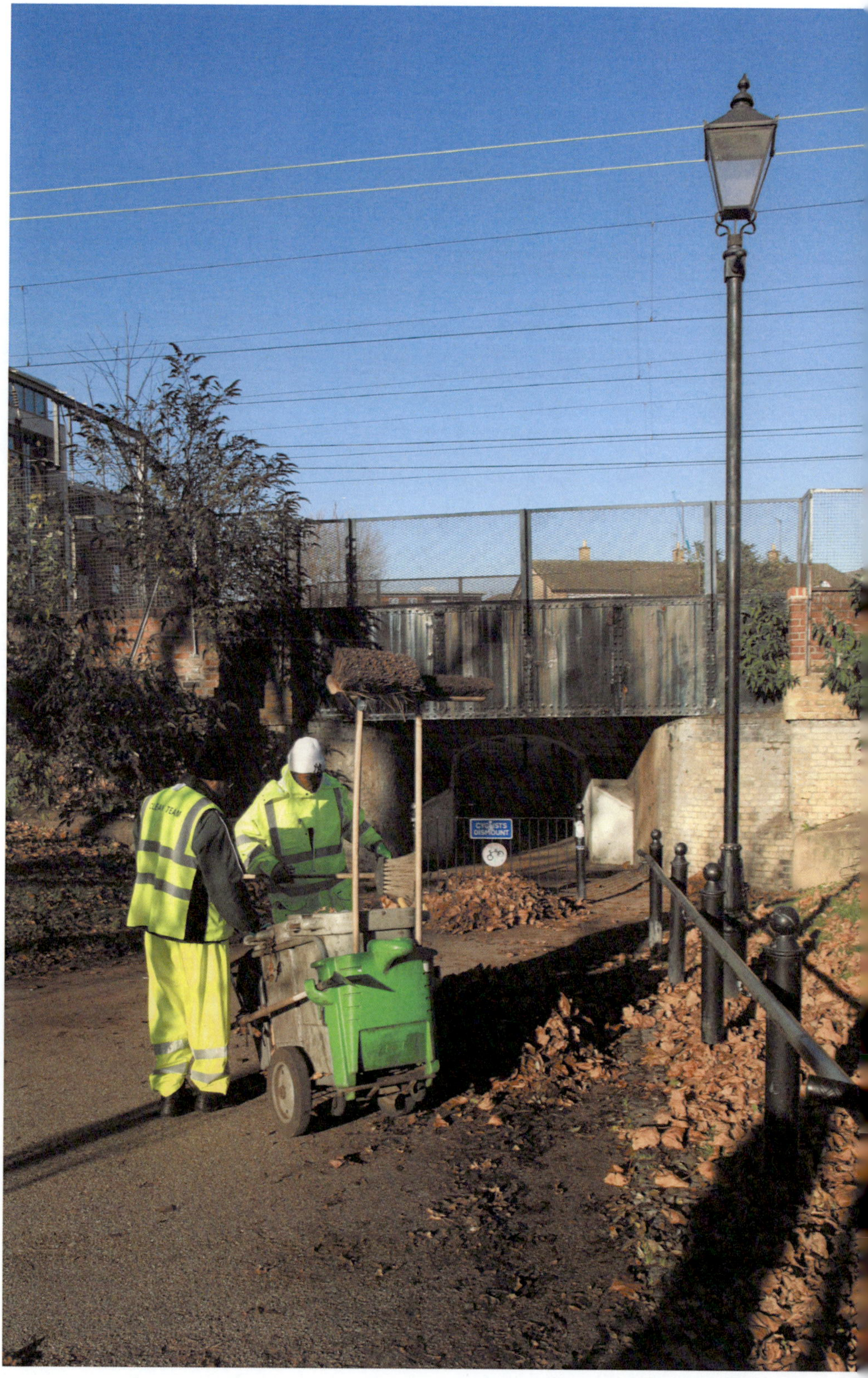
DISMOUNT
TEAM

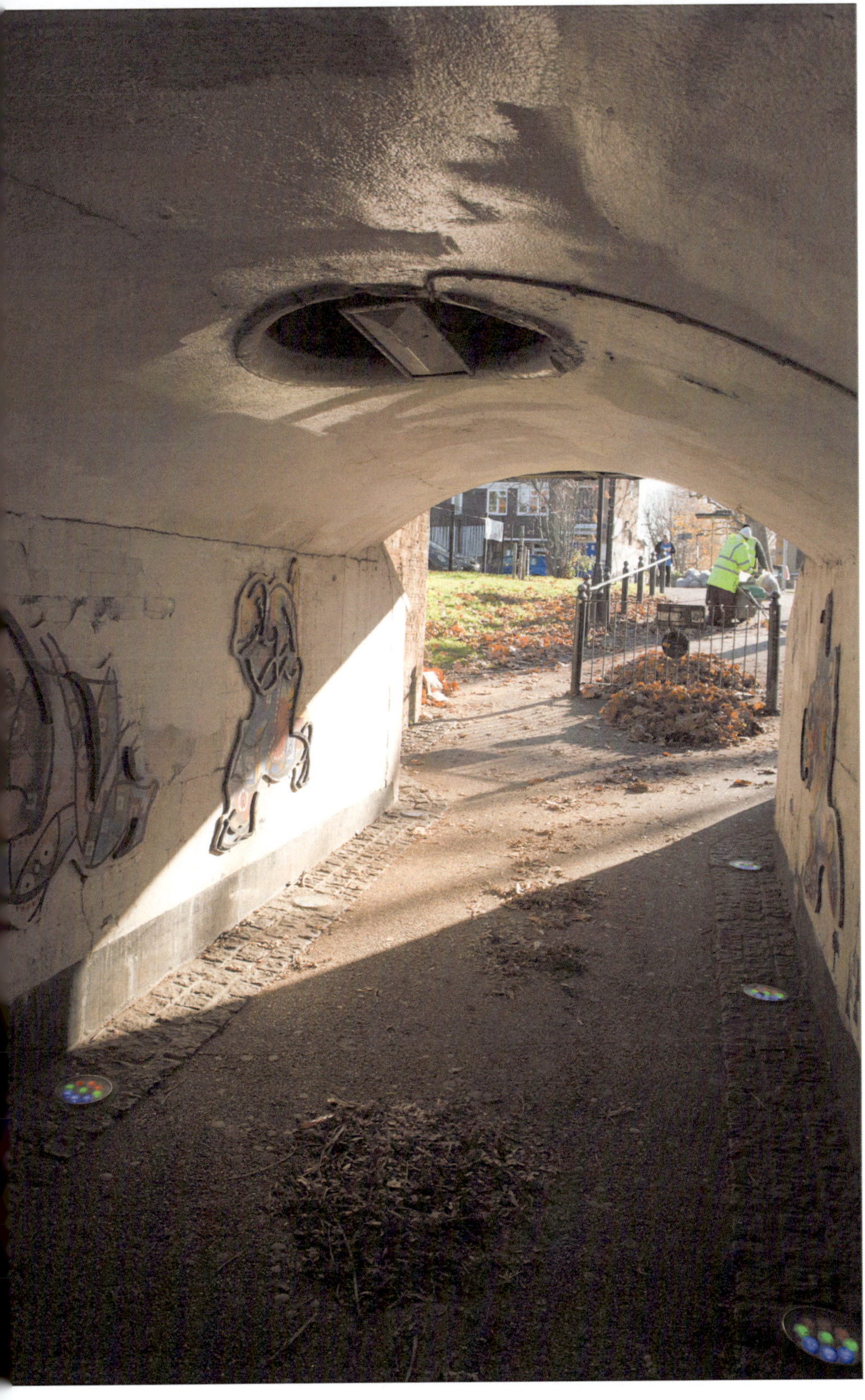

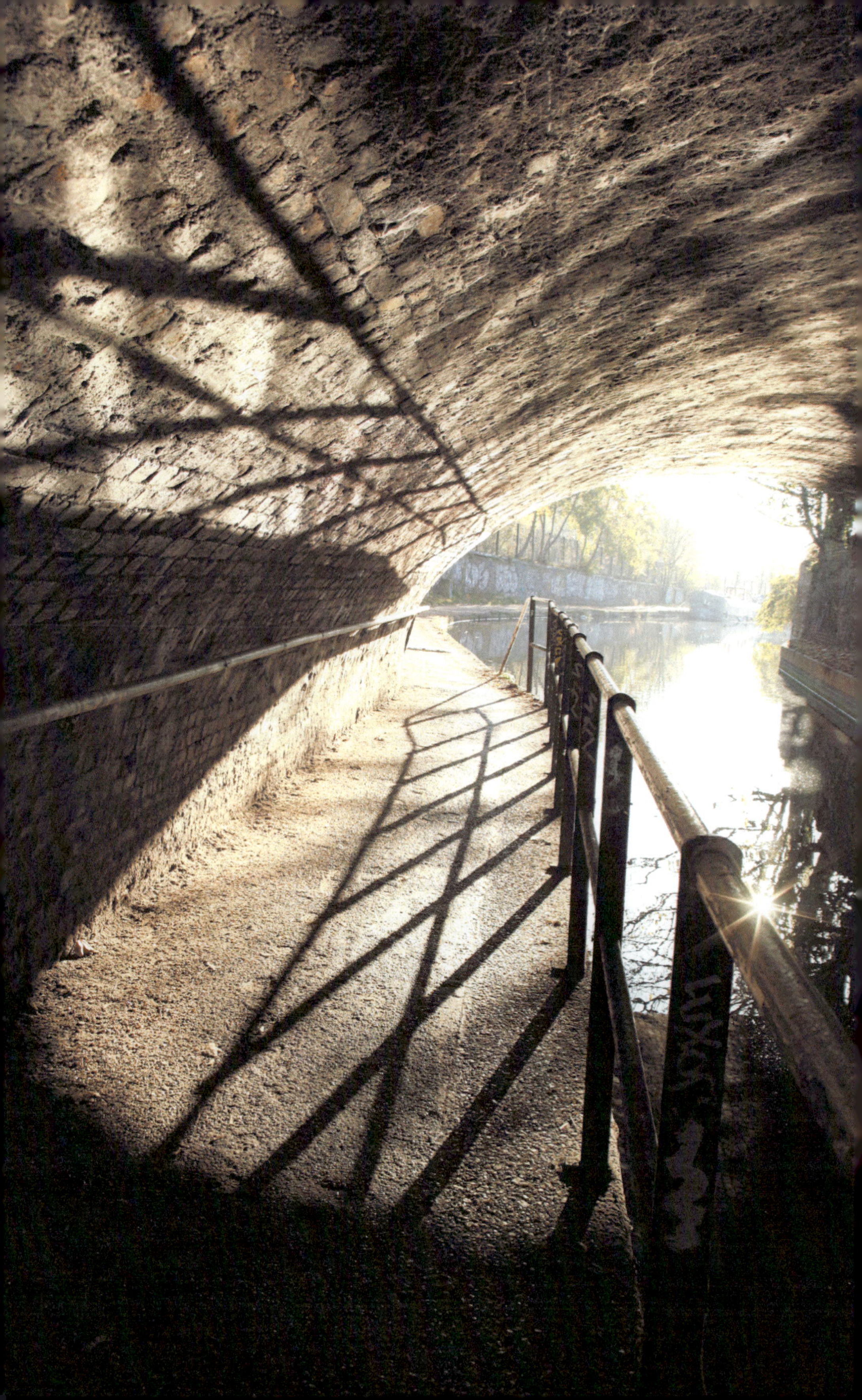

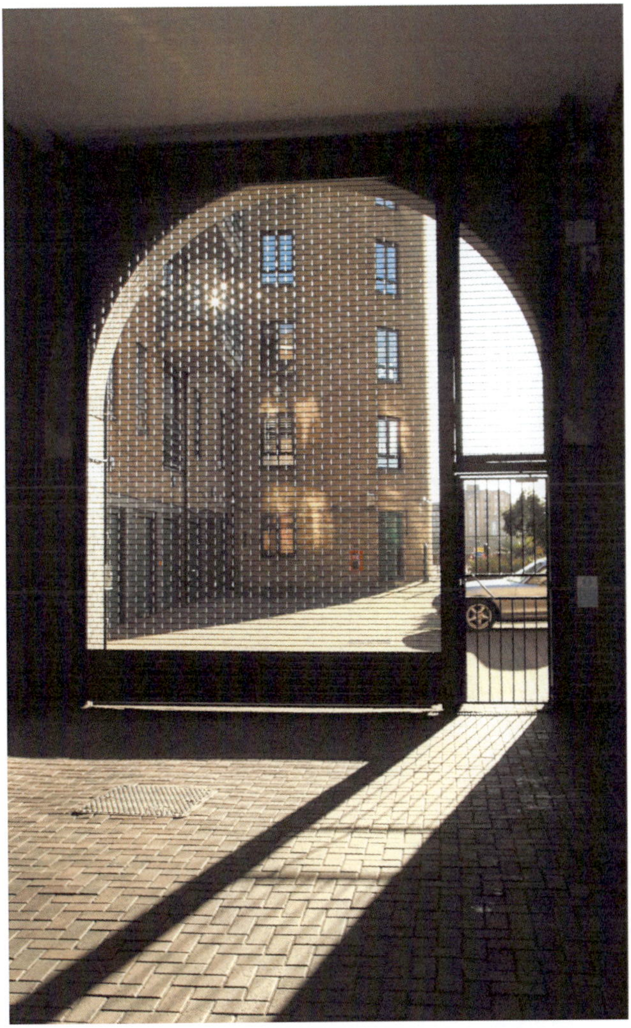

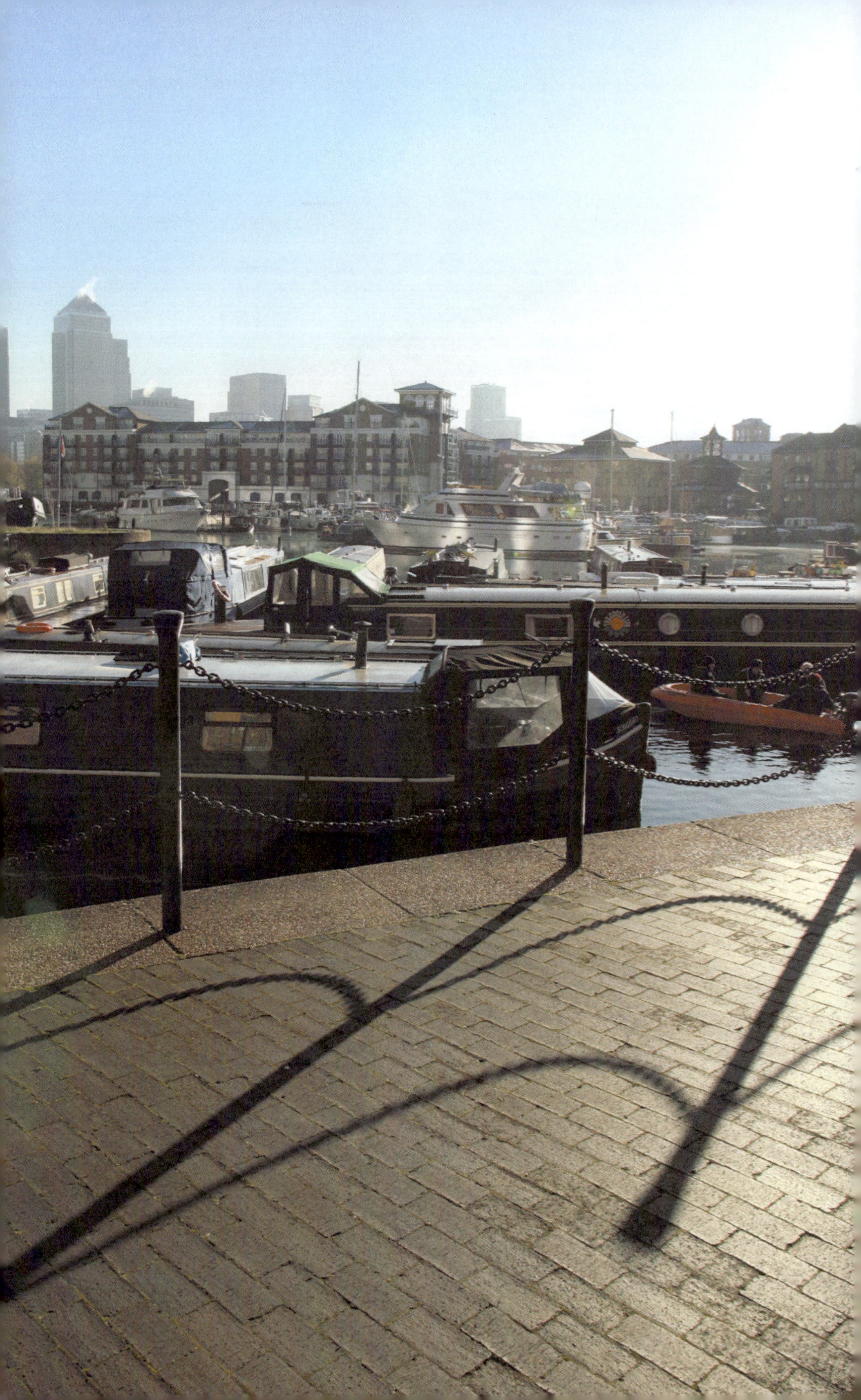

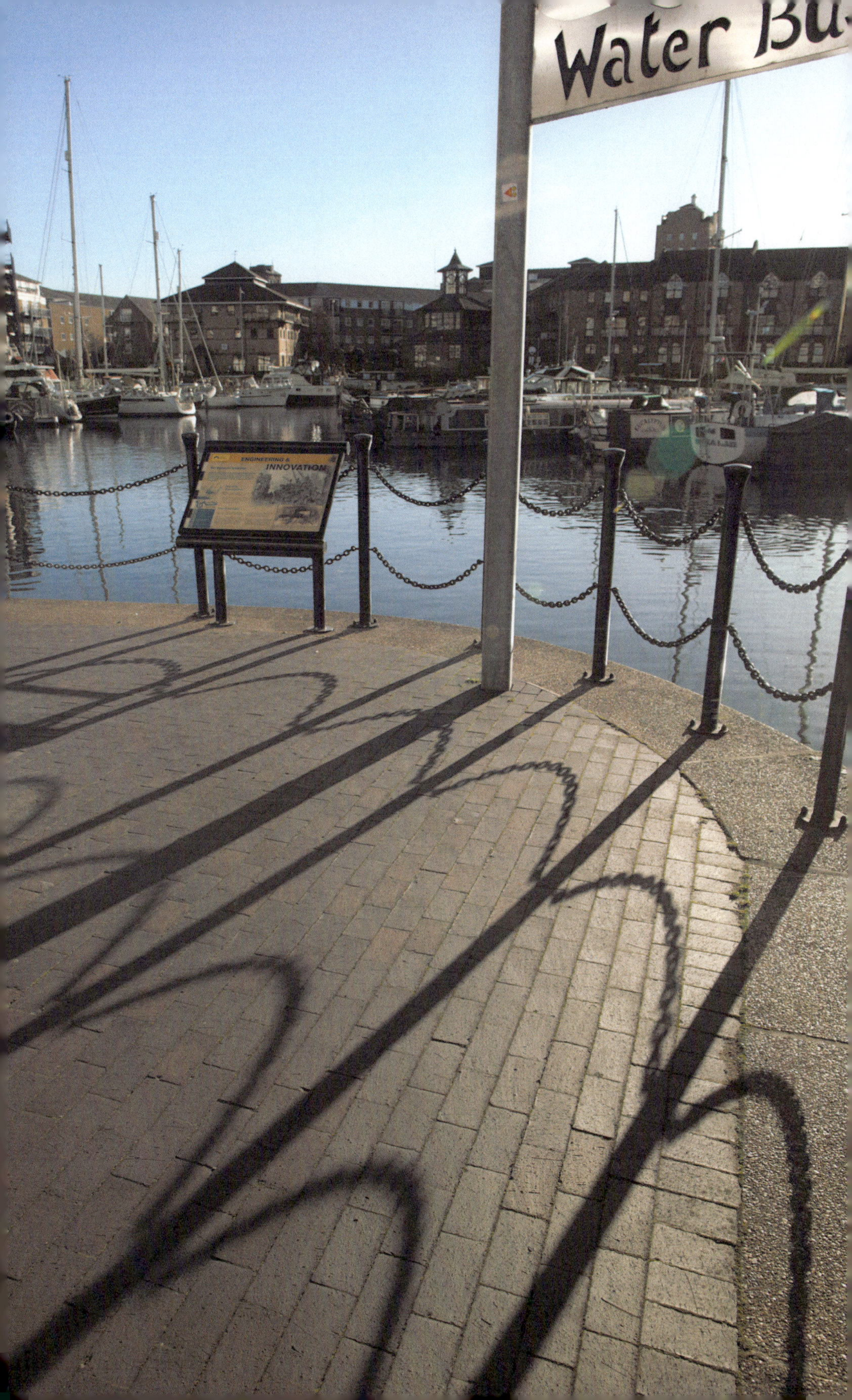
Water
ENGINEERING &
INNOVATION

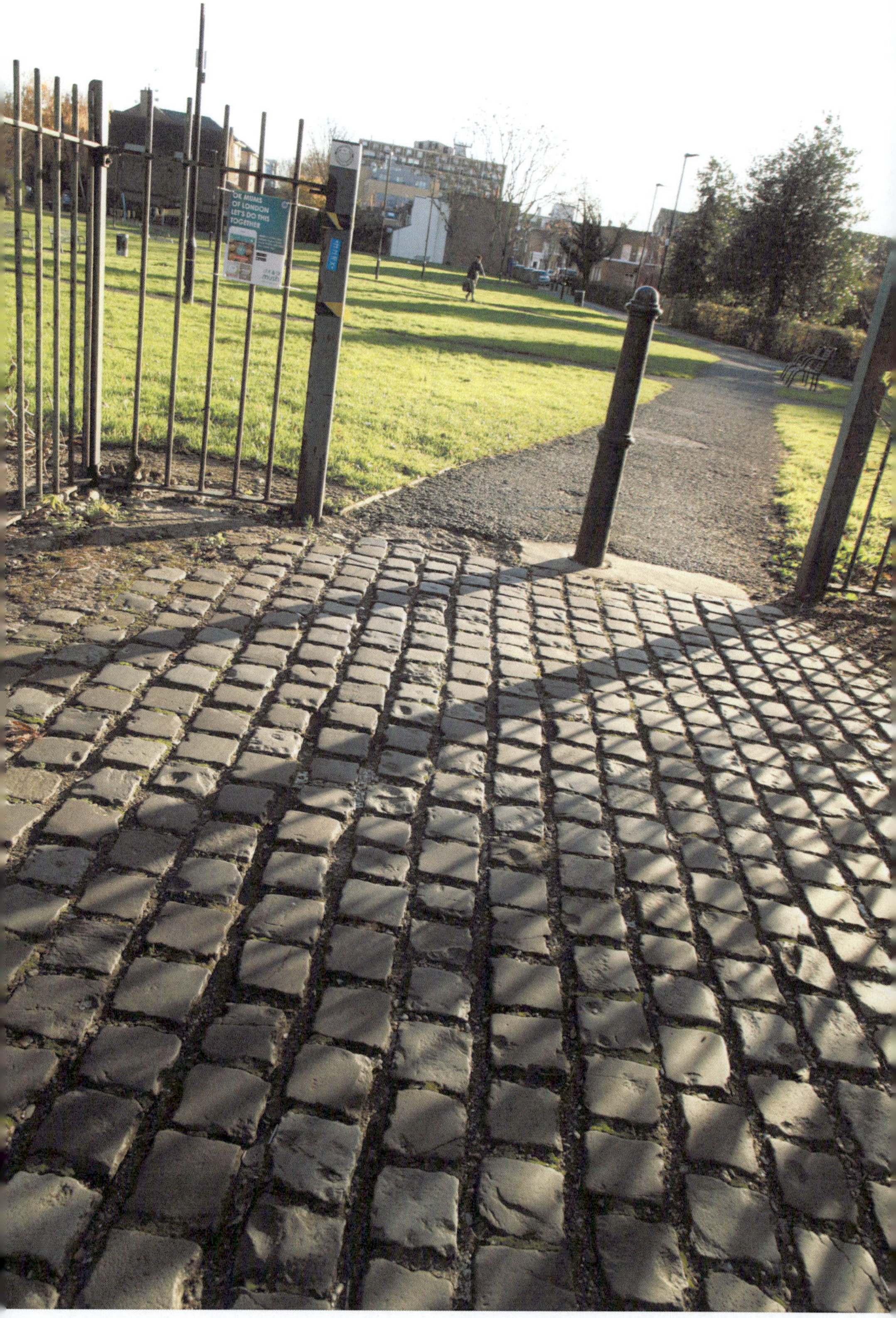
OK MUMS
OF LONDON
LET'S DO THIS
TOGETHER

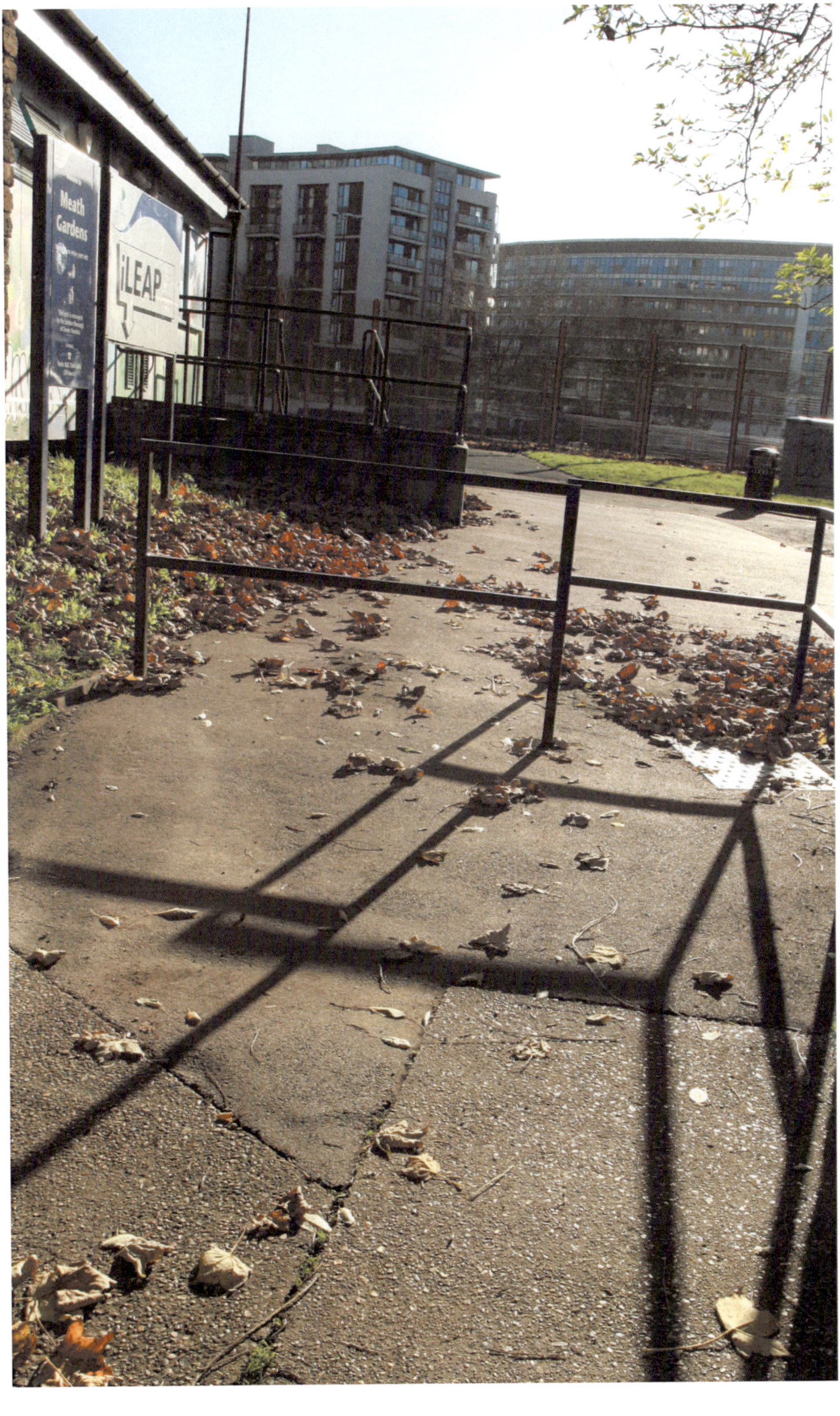
Meath Gardens
iLEAP

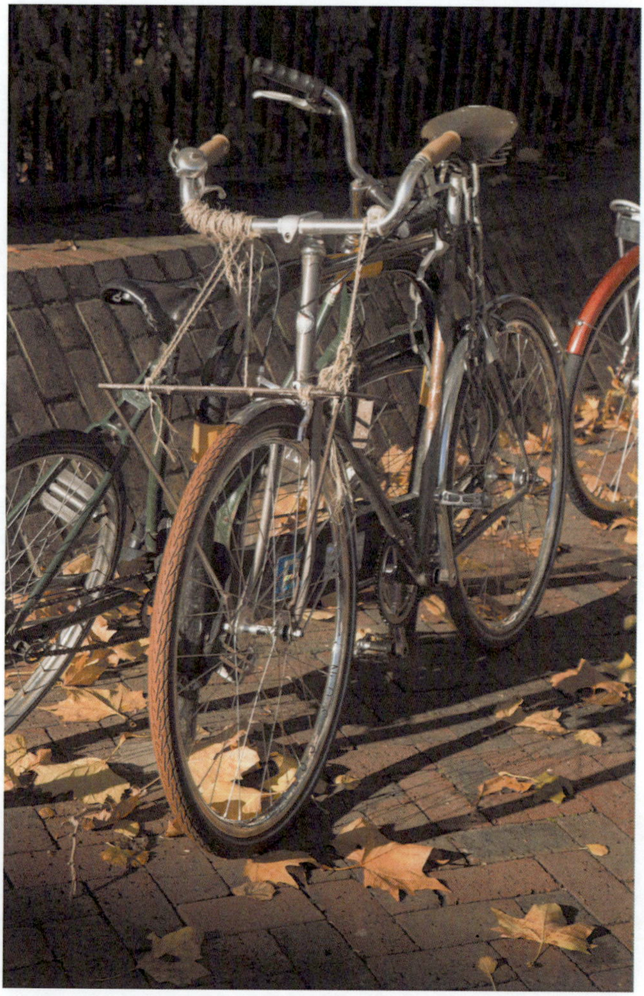

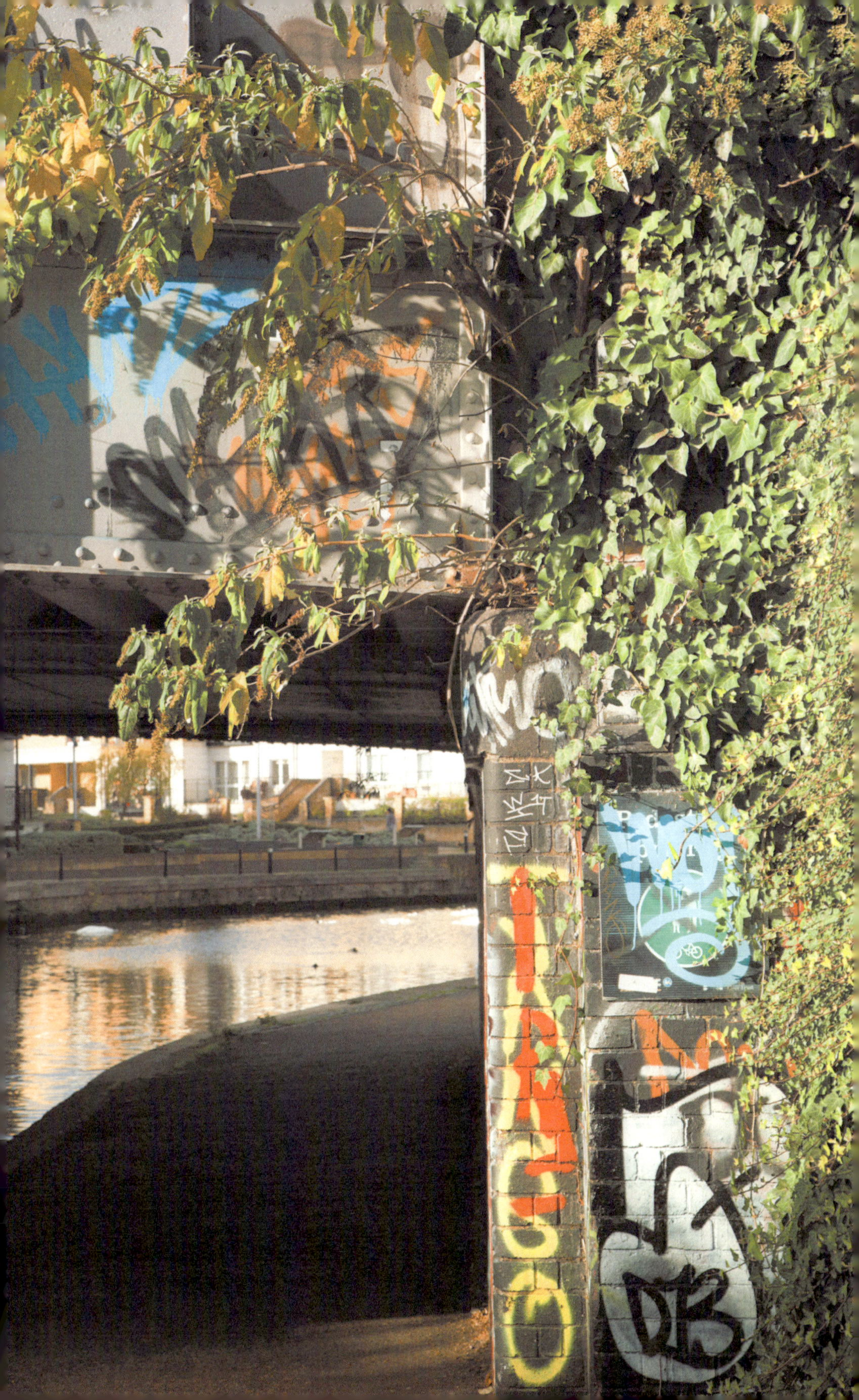

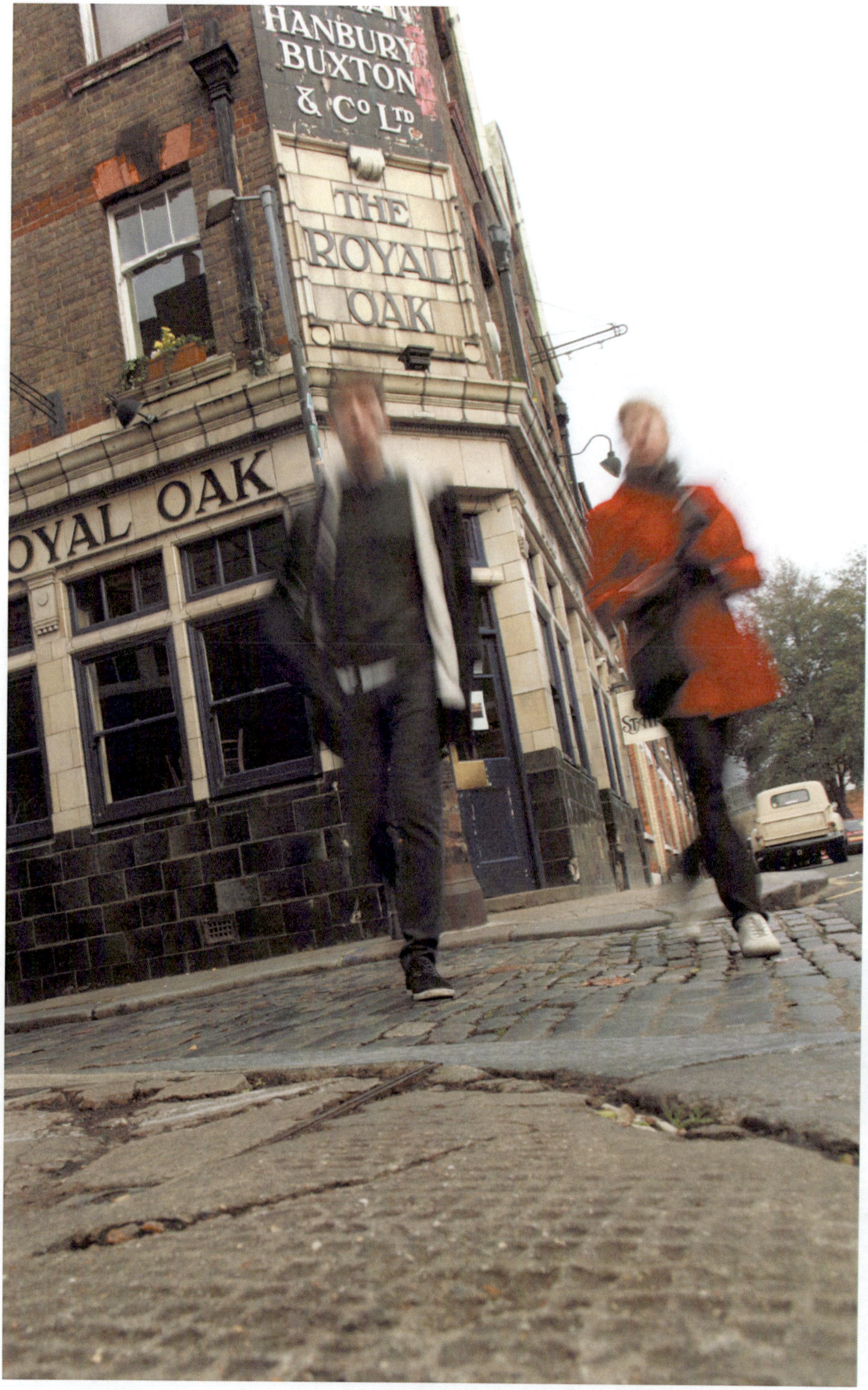
HANBURY
BUXTON
& Co Ltd
THE
ROYAL
OAK
ROYAL OAK

THE NOTEBOOK OF RICHARD NEWMAN OF MILE END NEW TOWN

Richard Newman's second wife, Elizabeth Reynolds *"came to me on August 1st, 1787"*. They were married at St. Bride's Fleet Street on October 21st and she died less than 5 years later, on May 18th, 1792, the last date referred to in his notes. Their troubles are recorded meticulously and many instances are given similar to the above. *"Thursday 12th February, 1789, my wife went away from me and took 4 guineas and stayed away 2 nights."; "November 12th 1790, my wife came home at 1 o'clock in the morn drunk with a man"; "Saturday 13th, Drunk again"*. The husband may have preferred to drink at home. His recipe for the Queen of Hungary's Cordial was :

1 pennyworth of Oil of Nutmeg
1 pennyworth of Oil of Cloves
1 pennyworth of Oil of Cinnamon
Mixt with 2 ozs of Castor Sugar then put q.v. into some best rum.

His cure for a cold was :

1 pint of Tent (i.e. Red wine)
1 pint of rum
1 pound of Turkey liggs chopped very small
1/2 pint of sweet oyle
Simmer them all up together to the consistence of an Electuary.
Take a teaspoonful 3 times a day.

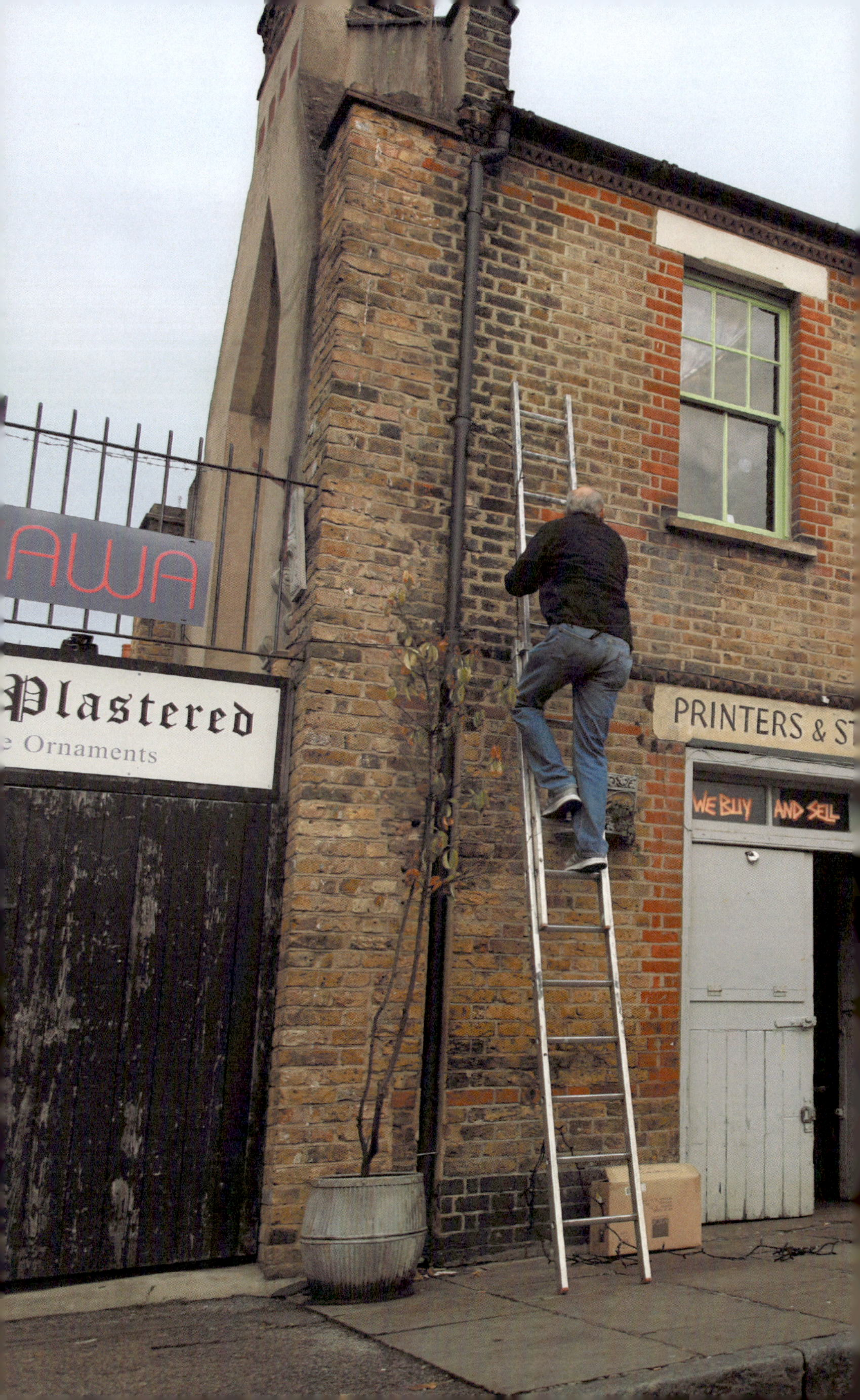
AWA
Plastered
e Ornaments
PRINTERS & ST
WE BUY
AND SELL

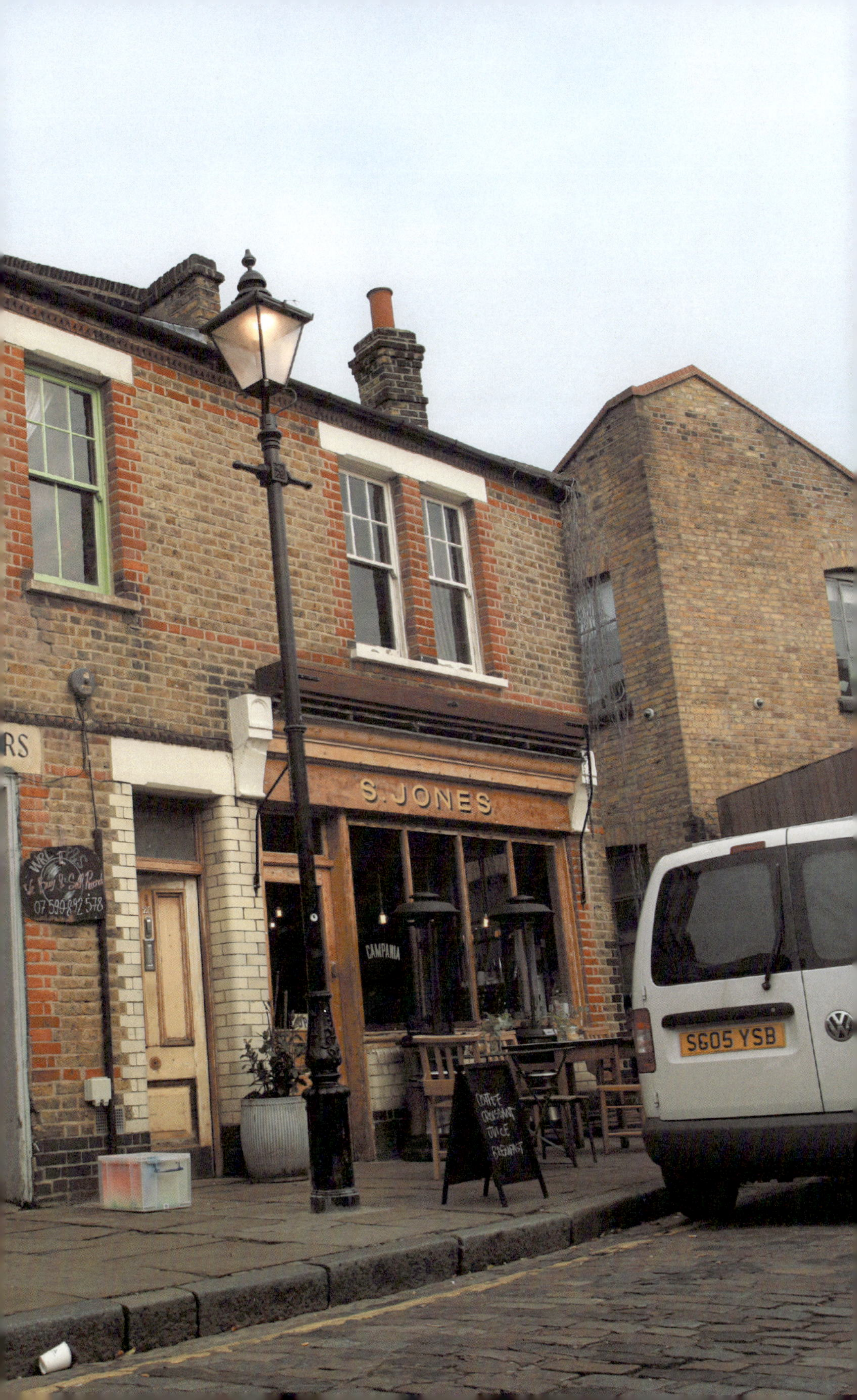
S. JONES
CAMPANIA

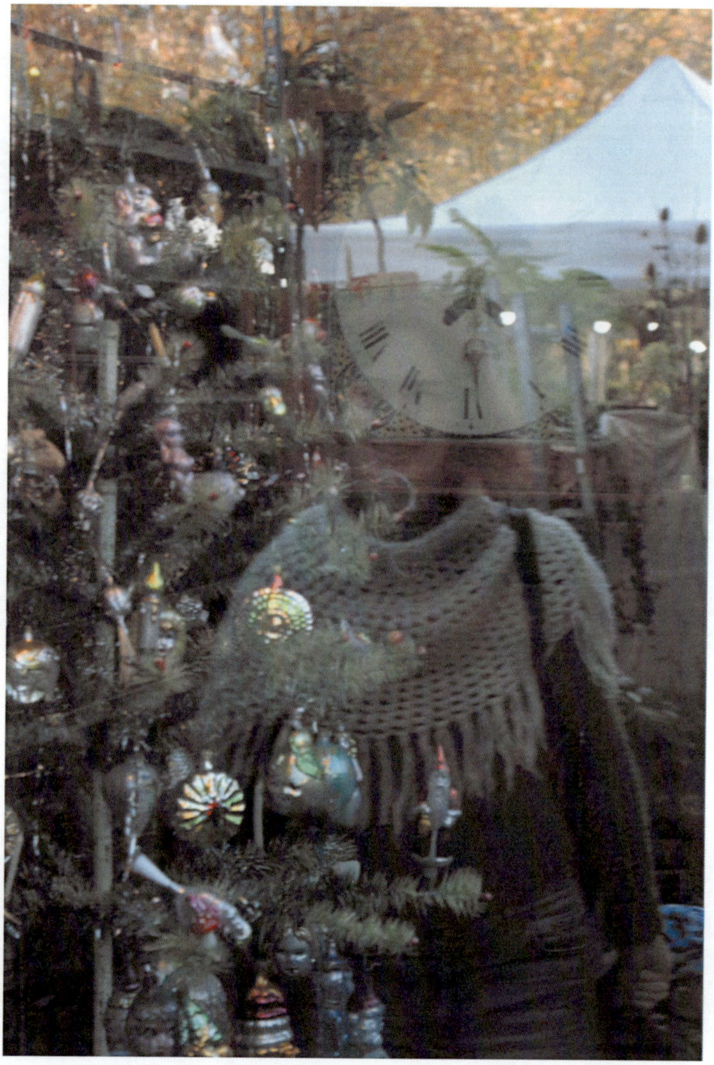

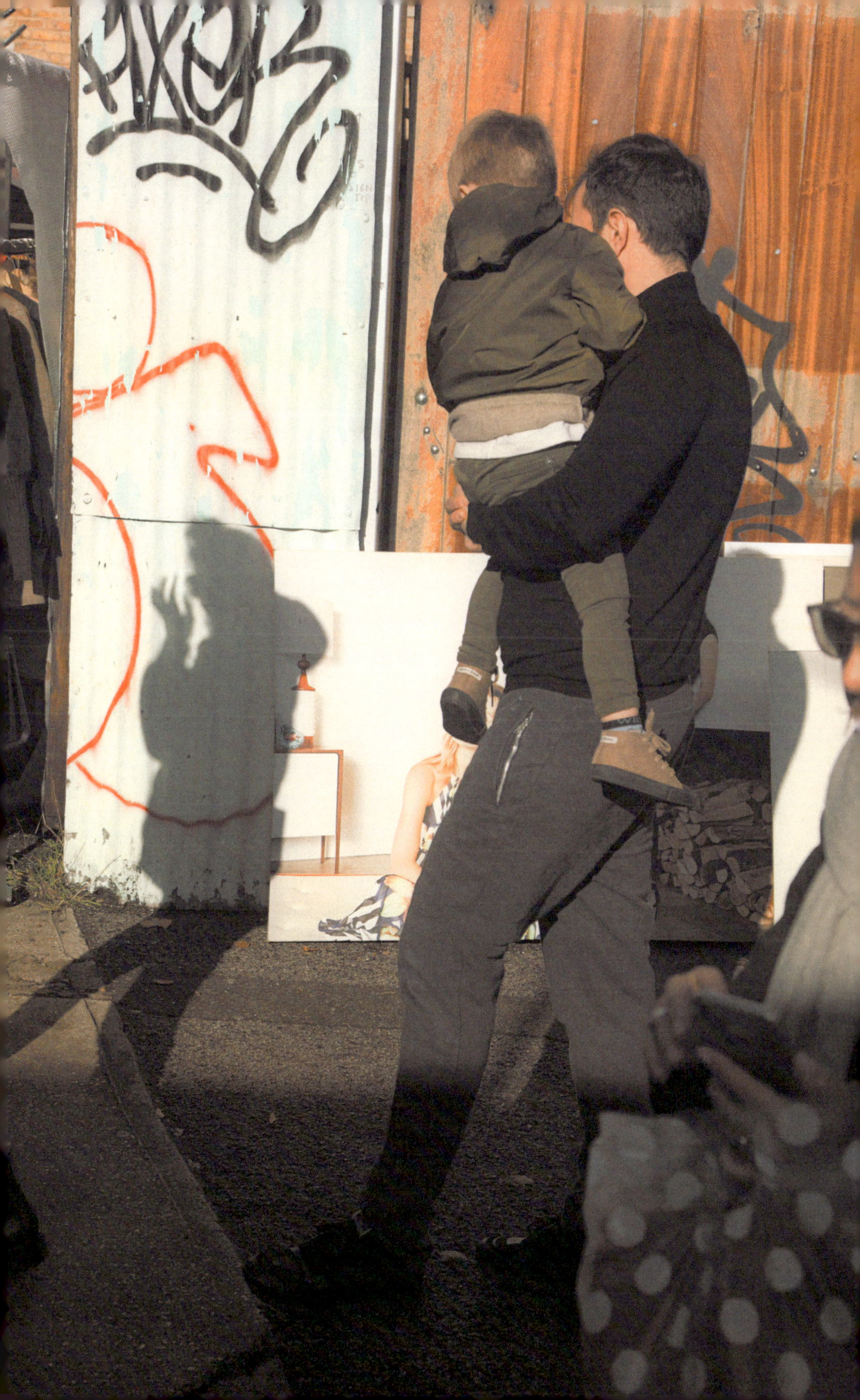

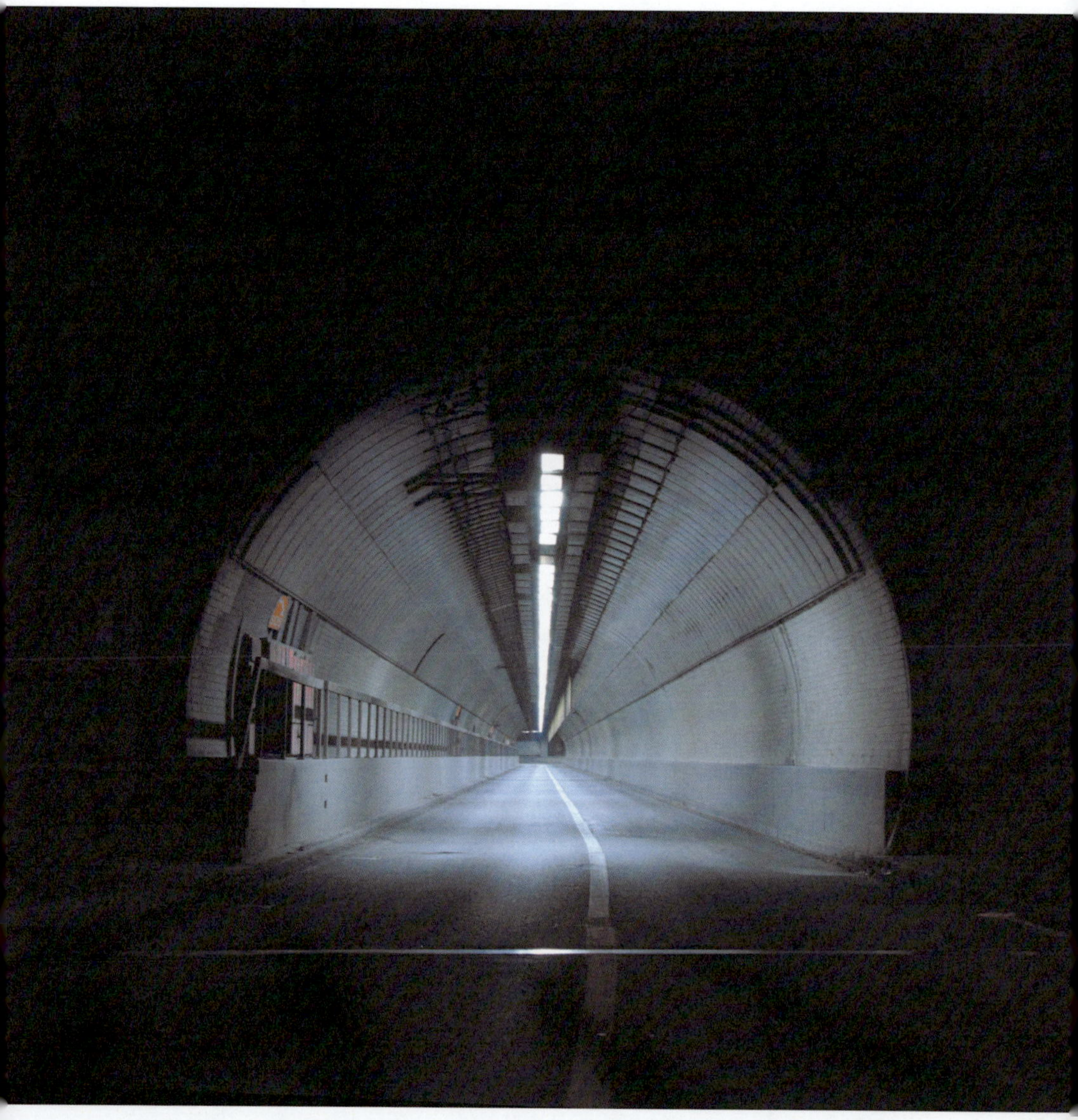

THE BLACKWALL TUNNEL HITCHHIKER

Although it is now forbidden to walk through the tunnel, it is claimed that on several occasions, drivers and especially motorcyclists, have swerved to avoid a walker.

The reason they say is that a man with long black hair and motorcycle gear is hitchhiking along the road by the tunnel's southern entrance. This particular tunnel just so happens to be the Victorian original.

One kindly driver pulled over to offer the young man a lift, The young man with long black hair accepted and jumped in and started telling them how he is about to meet his girlfriend nearby – and even gives a specific address as to where he is meeting his loved one. As the vehicle passes through the tunnel to the north side, the driver looks across to ask where the passenger might like to be dropped off – and is dumbfounded. The young man, that only a moment before sat in the back seat wearing motorcycle leathers, is not in the car but has mysteriously disappeared.

The driver is so concerned that he decided to drive to the nearby address the hitchhiker had given him. On arriving at the house and speaking with its resident, he was told that a young man matching his description did, in fact, once live at the house, but had been killed in a tragic motorcycle accident some years before...

A letter apparently appeared in the Times in 1994, in which a reader described an incident that took place in 1960. He had been staying in Blackwall Lane with his wife and father-in-law. When they were woken at 2am by the frightening sound of a massive crash. Later the following day, when residents came out to find out what happened, they learned of a motorcyclist being killed in the tunnel after a get-away gang that was being chased by police, went the wrong way.

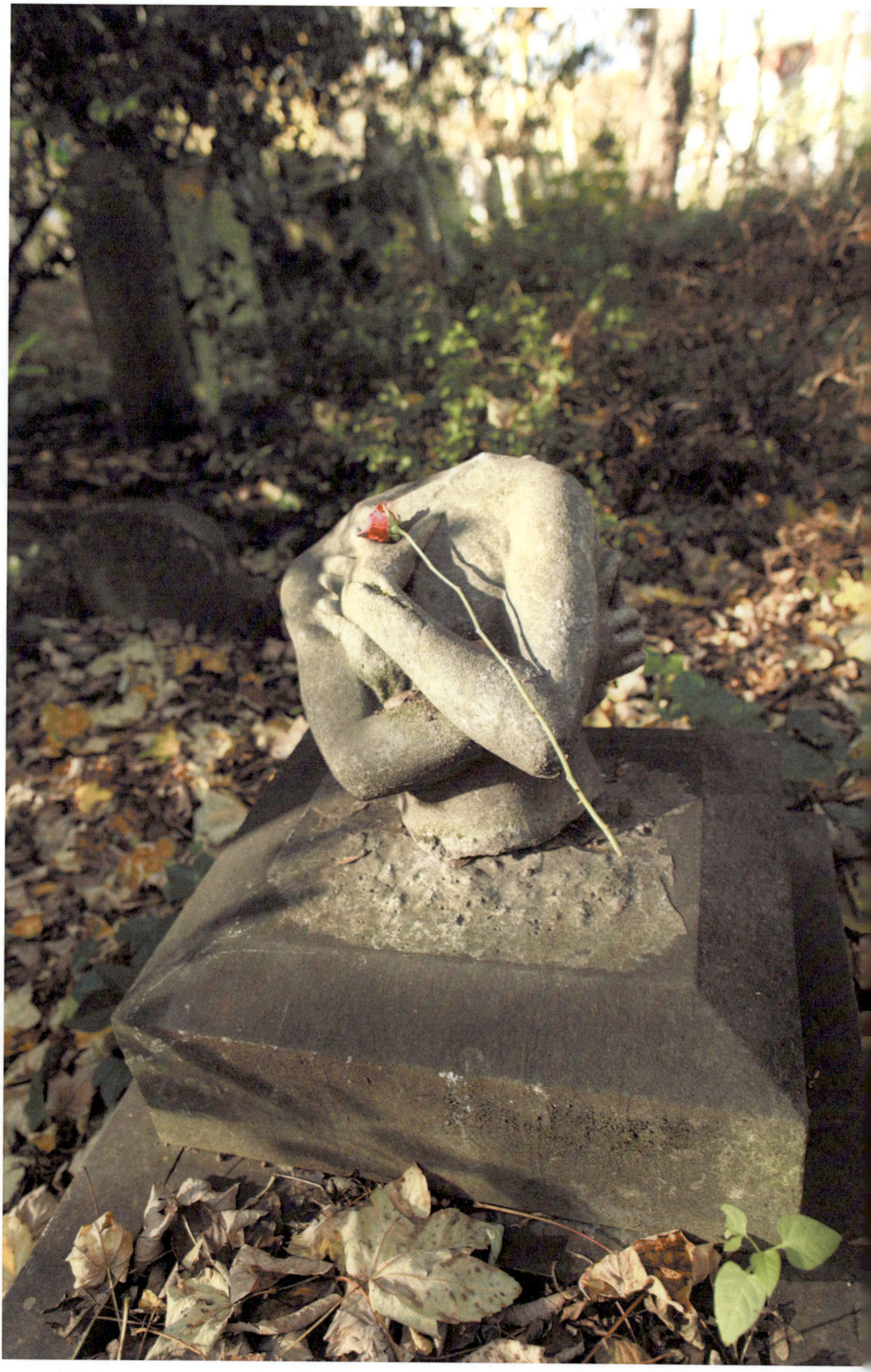

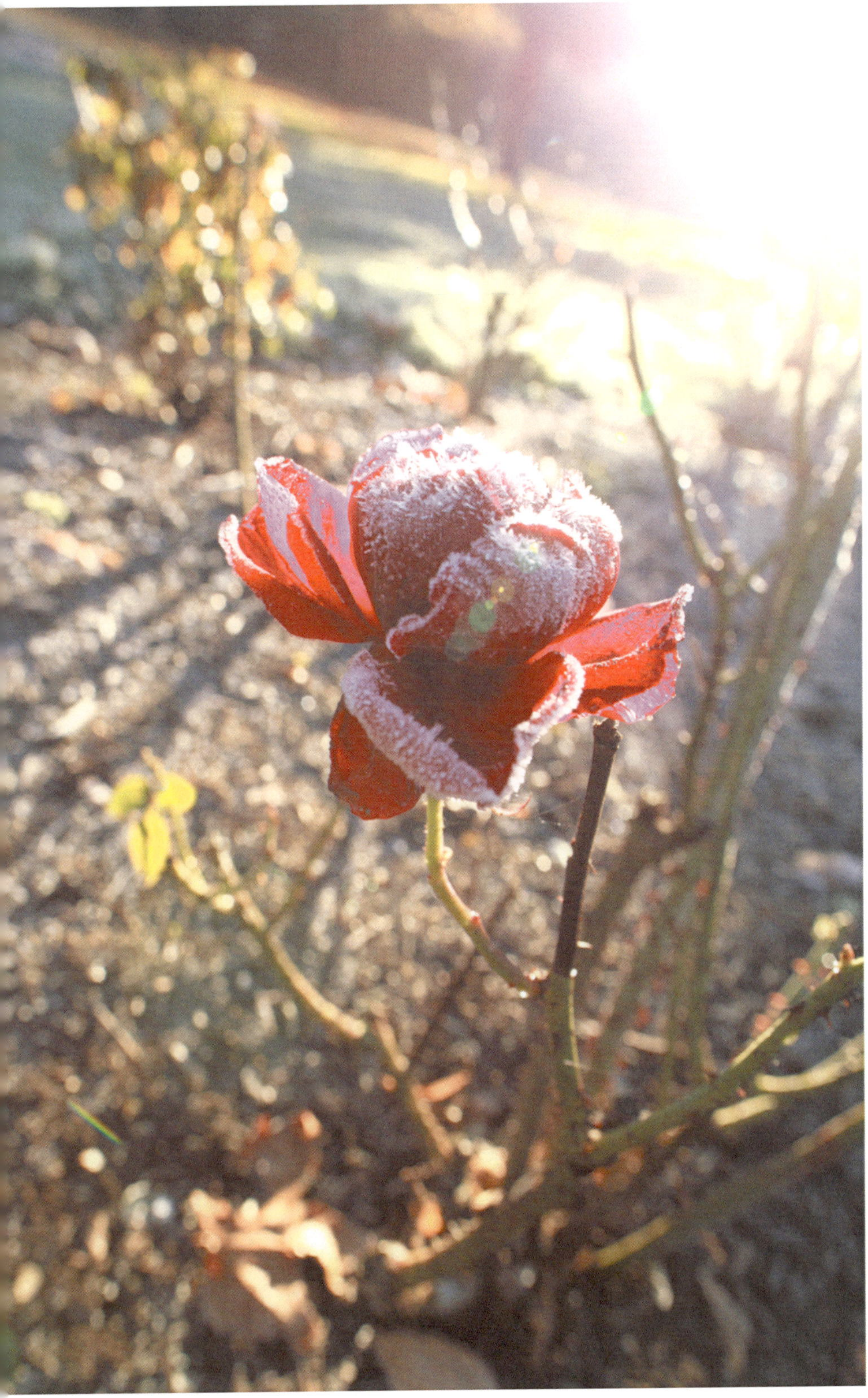

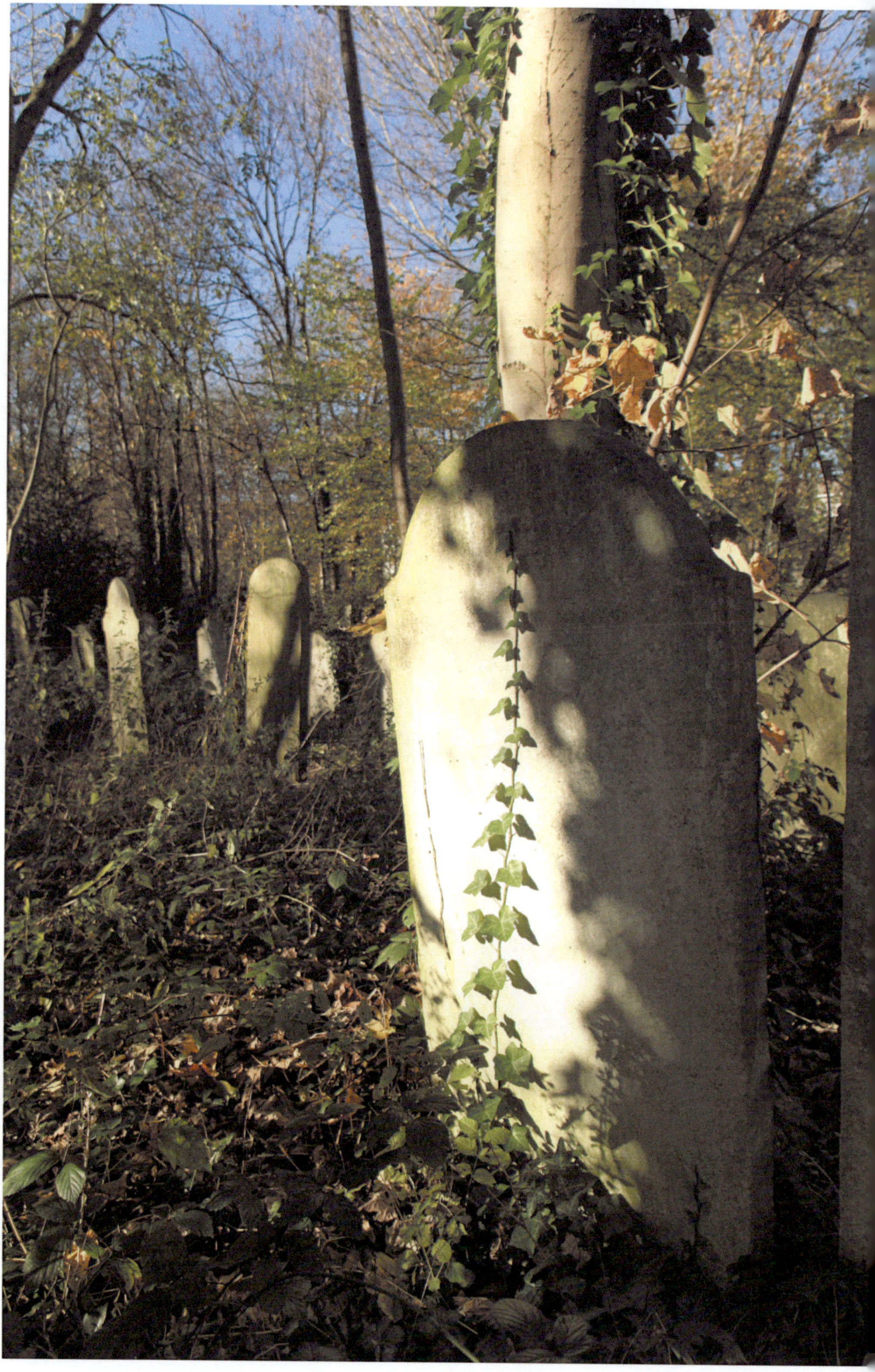

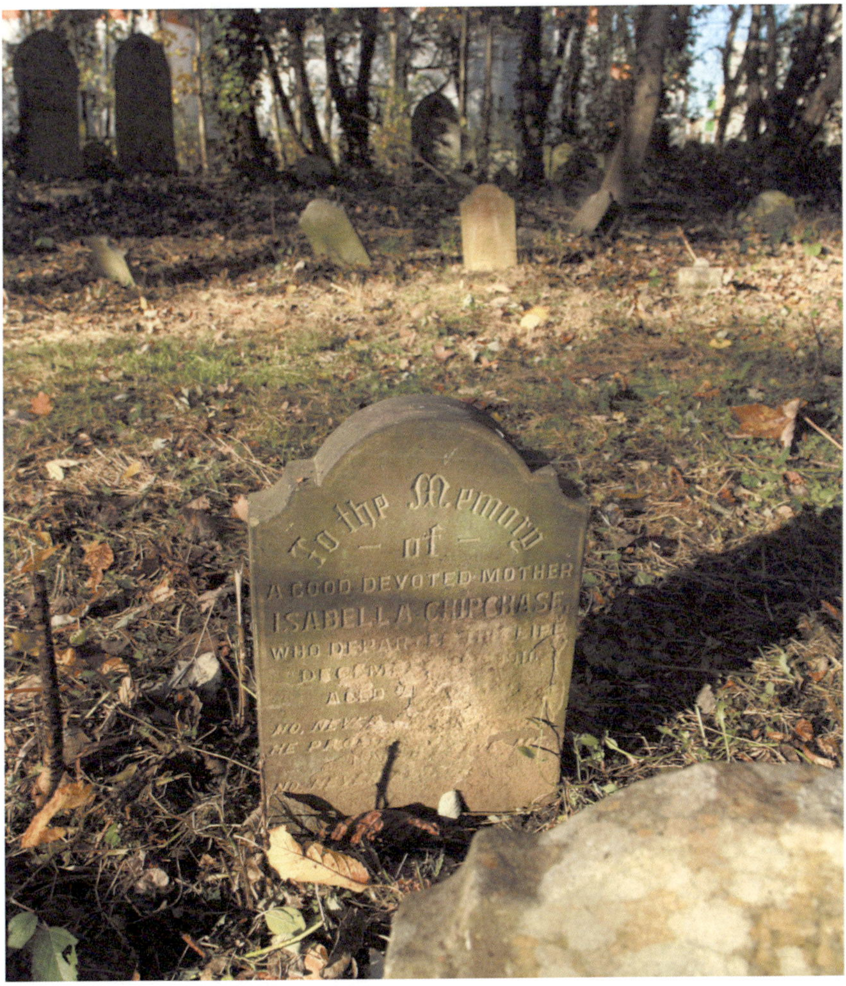
To the Memory
- of -
A GOOD DEVOTED MOTHER
ISABELLA CHURCHASE

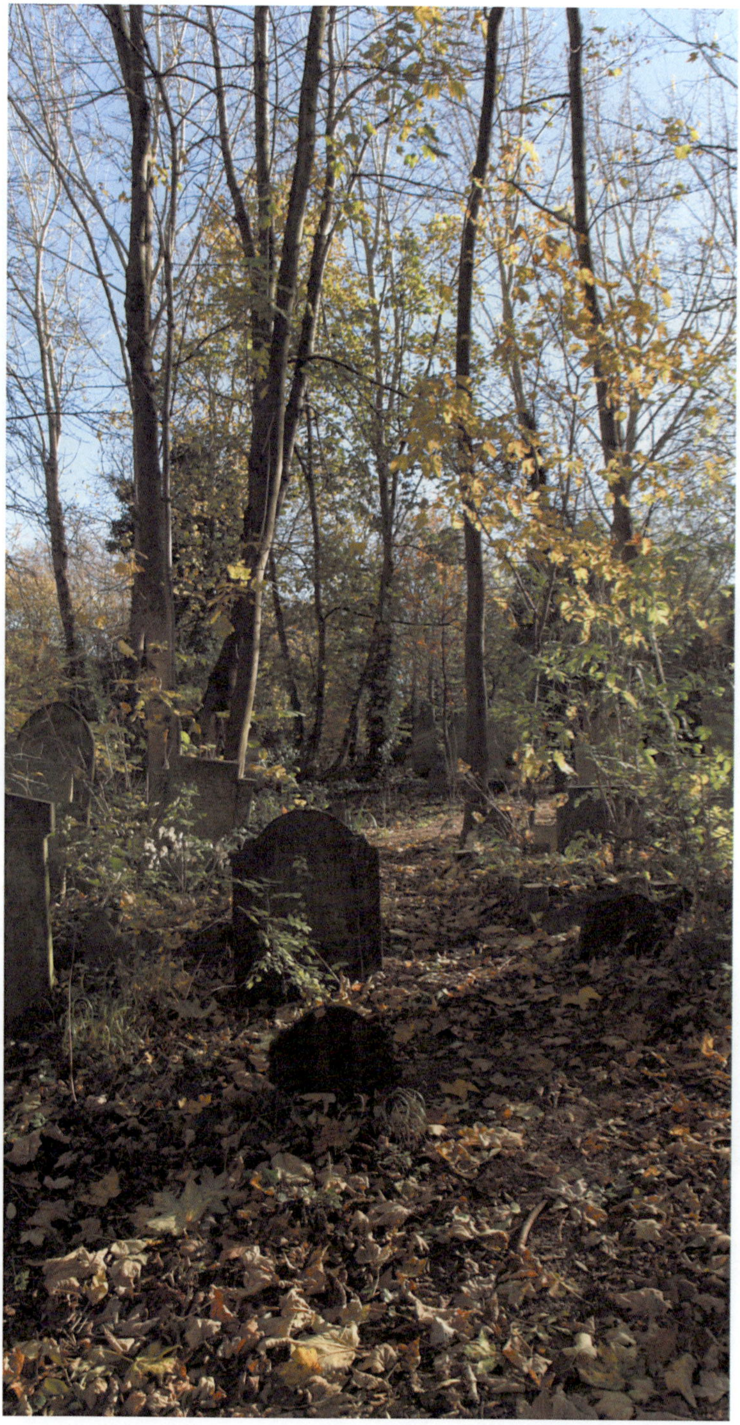

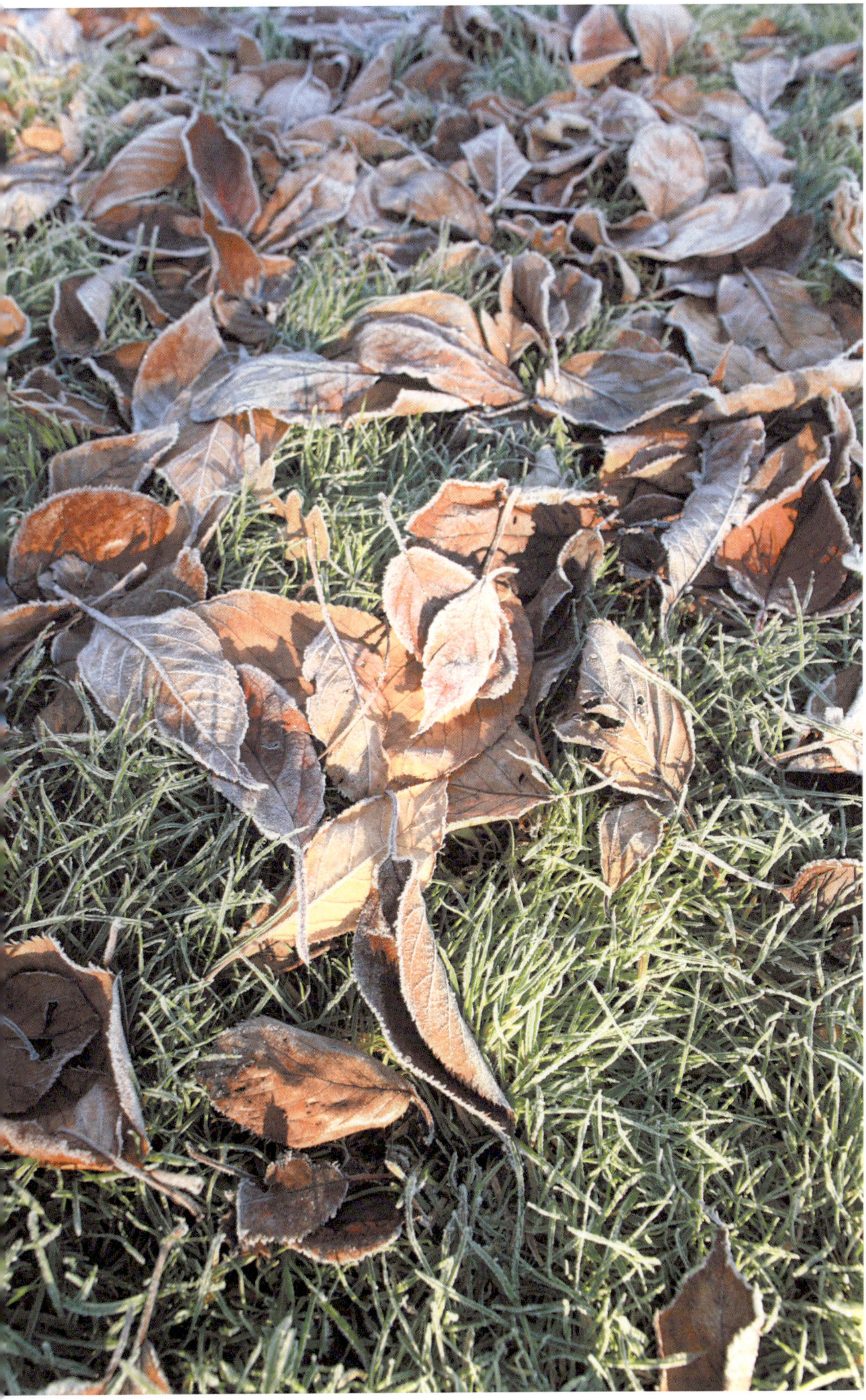

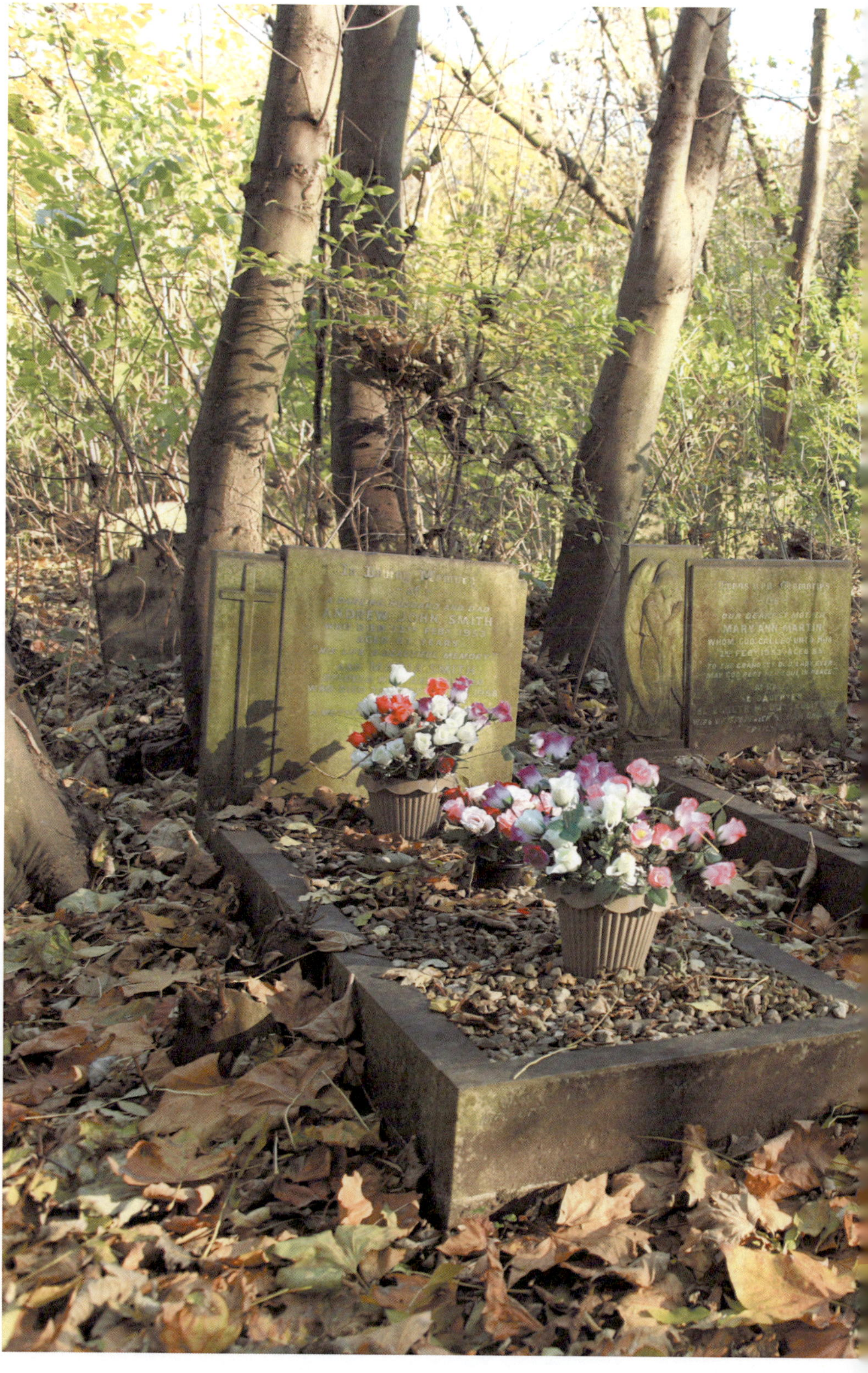
ANDREW JOHN SMITH
WHOM GOD CALLED UNTO HIM

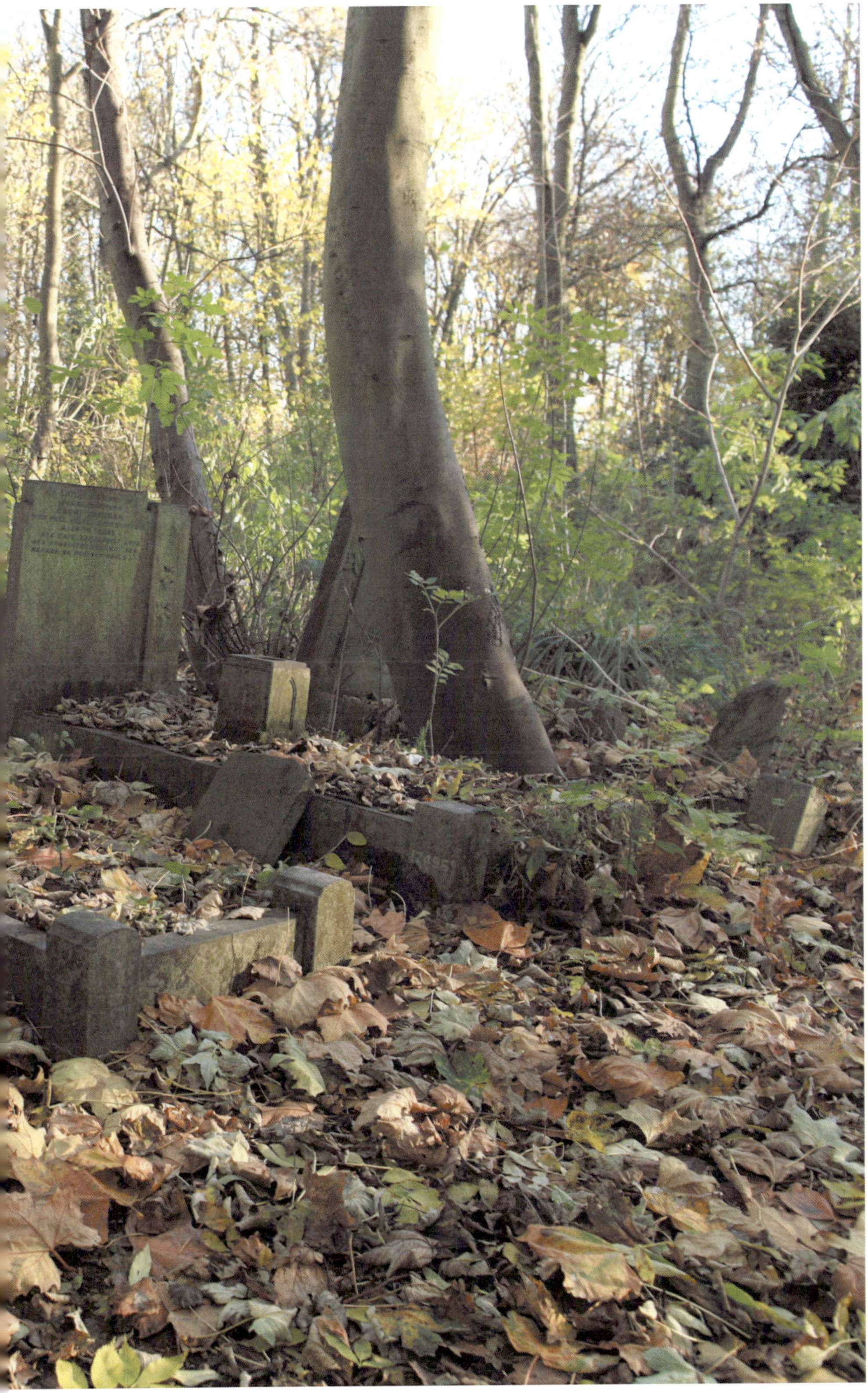

DICKENS AND THE CHINAMAN

According to an old acquaintance of the dead Chinaman, Ah Sing, 'was buried most comfortably'.

It had been claimed that since Ah Sing's death, his opium den was immortalised by Charles Dickens in the first chapter of 'The Mystery of Edwin Drood'. Ah Sing was always very proud to relate that his den had been visited by the great novelist – and Ah Sing's widow confirms that such a visit was made.

Dickens, in 'Edwin Drood,' certainly describes the court in which Ah Sing lived, but he describes the proprietor of the opium joint as a woman *"so hideous a woman that she could hardly have been Ah Sing's wife"*, for the latter is mild-mannered, soft-spoken, and rather pleasant-looking. In the story, this woman refers to *"Jack Chinaman t'other side of the court"* as the only person in the vicinity who, besides herself, possesses the true secret of mixing opium, adding, with an eye to business, *"but he can't do it as well as me"*.

At the grave, the Church of England burial service was read – Ah Sing had so wished – thereby showing that he had not renounced the worship of Joss, a figure of a traditional Chinese deity, purely for commercial reasons. His virtues and his trials were comfortably discussed over a hearty meal late on Sunday afternoon by the mourning neighbour and some visitors who had called to condole with Ah Sing's widow.

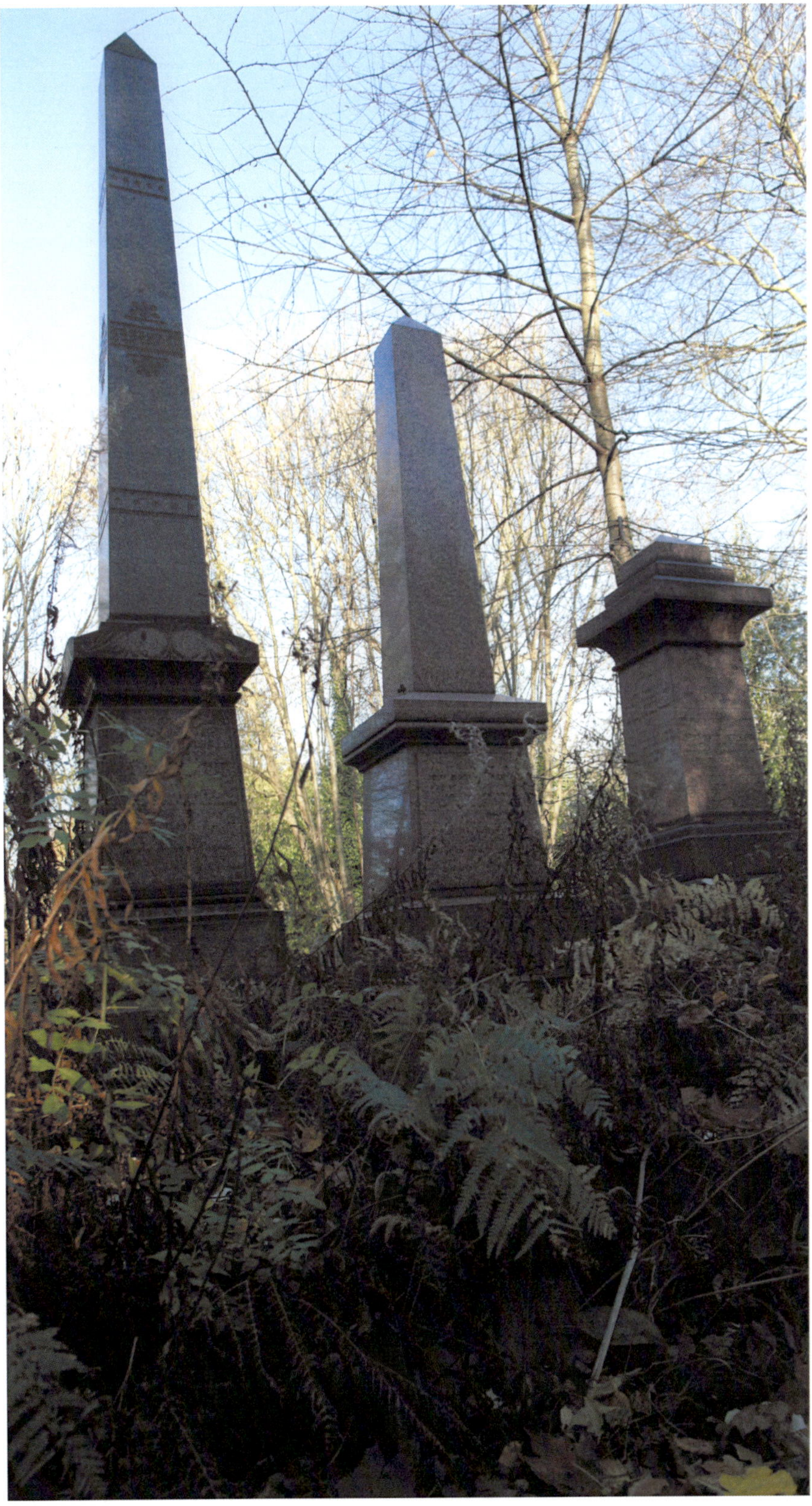

CAUGHT IN THE JAWS OF A BENGAL TIGER

The Thames, a pipe line for the world of wonders, brought many exotic trading ships to the doorstep of London – and with it a conundrum of enterprising merchants.

With the birth of London Zoo in Regents Park, there was introduced a passion for exotic animals. Mr Charles Jamrach, was a dealer in birds, shells and wildlife, of the Ratcliffe Highway in East London. His menagerie contained a Bengal Tiger, a rare and terrifying animal imported to entertain and quench the public's insatiable desire to see such dangerous, exotic curiosities.

But, unfortunately, during the chilling month of October 1857, the newly acquired Tiger managed to escape.

By Mr Jamrach's account, *"The Tiger, in putting his forepaws against the iron bars in front of the den, had exerted his full strength to push with his back against the boards behind, and had thus succeeded in gaining his liberty.*

"As soon as he got into the street, a boy of about nine years of age put out his hand to stroke the beast's back, when the tiger seized him by the shoulder and ran down the street with the lad hanging in his jaws. My men had been seized with the same panic as the bystanders, but now I discovered one lurking round a corner, so I shouted to him to come with a crowbar; he fetched one, and hit the tiger three tremendous blows over the eyes and rendered it unconscious".

However after the incident, Mr. Edmonds, proprietor of Whitwell Menagerie, having read the report in the papers, came up to town post haste, and paid £300 for the Tiger. He exhibited him as *"The Tiger that swallowed the Child"*, and by all accounts made a small fortune with him.

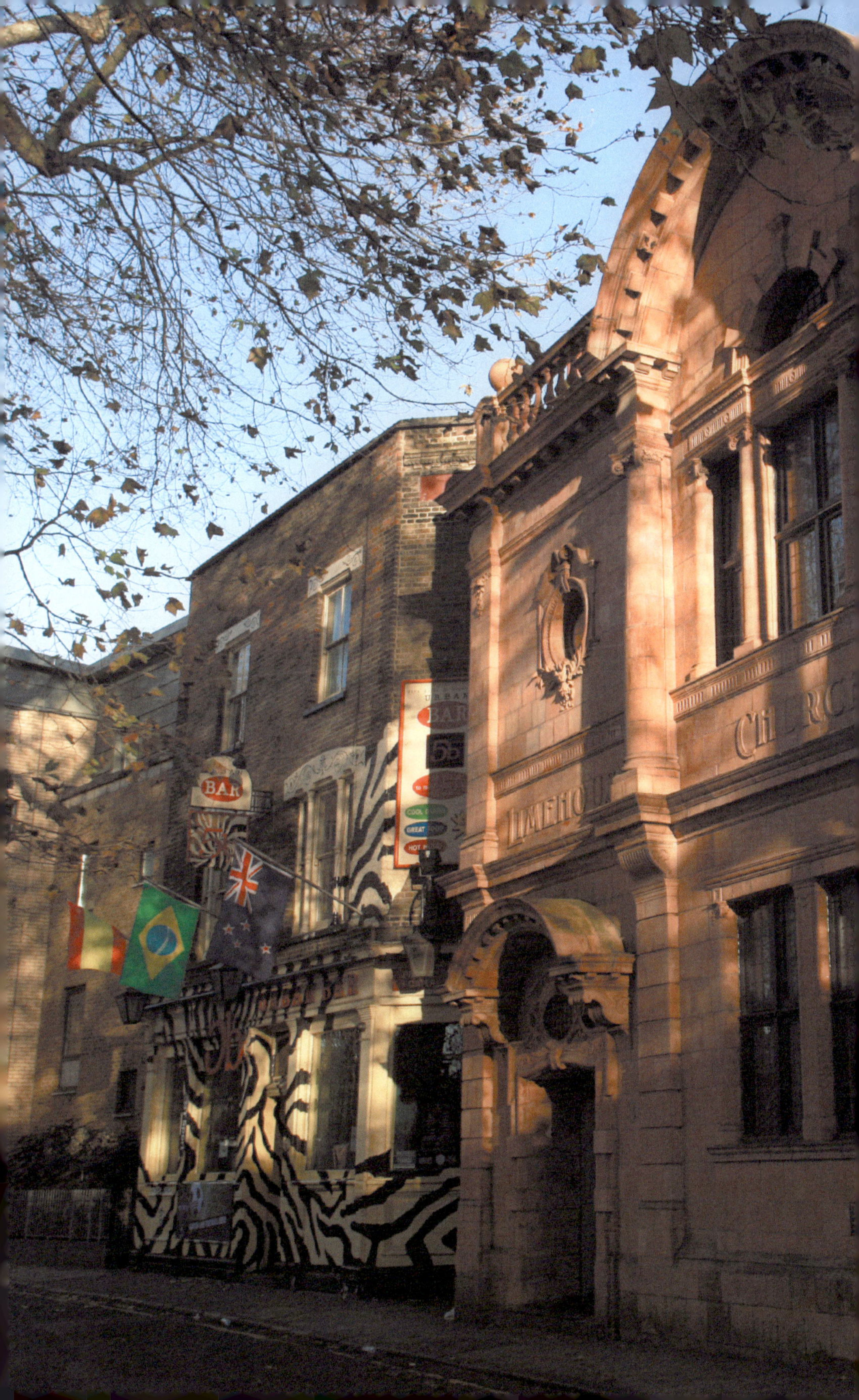
BAR

OTHER BOOKS BY THE AUTHOR

> Little London Adventures & Cockney Curiosities
< Little London Adventures & Poultry Passages
> Little London Adventures & Shady Shadwell
< Little London Adventures & Titillating Thames

CLARE NEWTON FRSA

Awarded British Female Inventor of the Year and a Fellow at the Royal Society of Arts.

One of Clare's many endeavours was an extraordinary project called 'Jump4London', to celebrate London 2012. She made the World's Longest Photograph, with 5,000 people taking part and appearing to simultaneously jump. True to form it made a Double Guinness World Record as part of the Cultural Olympiad's World Record London – it was an astonishing 1 kilometre long by 2 metres high, printed on two and a half tons of specialist photographic material, used a swimming pool's amount of ink and took 29 days, 24/7 to print continuously.

I hope you enjoyed this curious photographic journey. If you have, would you be so kind as to leave a review on the site where you bought the book.

Much appreciated

VERY HELPFUL SOURCES

Cockney Rhyming Slang By Nigel T Espey

Chaucer's Reeve's Tale and its Old French Analogue by Mary MacArthy

Victorian Costermongers: "A Penny Profit out of the Poor Man's Dinner" by Dick Sullivan

Victorian Back Slang by Dick Sullivan

The Hitchcock Zone &

Smallest canal becomes the shortest, conversations with the local fishermen and lock-keeper's great grandson

The life of Jane Shore by David Crowther

The curious death of poet Edmund Spenser by John Rennie

www.newworldencyclopedia.org/entry/Luis_de_Gongora - "A man to a nose was glued"

www.classicspanishbooks.com/16th-cent-baroque-quevedo.html

Sir William Henry Perkin and the Coal-Tar Colours by Jacqueline Banerjee PhD

How The Colour Purple Was Invented In London by Laurence Scales

Mile End and the fraternity of Longbow Archers longbow-archers.com/prince.html

The Notebook of Richard Newman by members of The East London History Society

Phantom Hitchhiker by Icy Sedgwick

The East London Observer (a local paper from 1857)

www.mernick.org.uk/thhol/curiousburial.html

www.mernick.org.uk/thhol/jamrach.html

HAPPY LONDON PRESS

www.ingramcontent.com/pod-product-compliance
Ingram Content Group UK Ltd.
Pitfield, Milton Keynes, MK11 3LW, UK
UKRC031011310726
14089UKWH00013B/249